SI

NOTES

including
- *Biography and Background of the Author*
- *Brief Synopsis of the Novel*
- *List of Characters*
- *Chapter Summaries and Commentaries*
- *Character Analyses*
- *Critical Analysis of the Novel*
- *Questions for Review*
- *Selected Bibliography*

by
William Holland,
Rhodes Scholar

NEW EDITION

INCORPORATED

LINCOLN, NEBRASKA 68501

Editor	Consulting Editor
Gary Carey, M.A.	*James L. Roberts, Ph.D.*
University of Colorado	*Department of English*
	University of Nebraska

ISBN 0-8220-1192-1
© Copyright 1966
by
C. K. Hillegass
All Rights Reserved
Printed in U.S.A.

1989 Printing

Cliffs Notes, Inc.   Lincoln, Nebraska

CONTENTS

Silas Marner

BIOGRAPHY AND BACKGROUND

George Eliot was the pen name of Mary Ann (later Marian) Evans, who was born in a country house at Nuneaton, Warwickshire, in 1819. The plains and hedges of her native region furnish the setting of many of her novels, including *Silas Marner*. With her sister Mary Ann attended two boarding schools for girls, where she was strongly influenced by evangelical Christianity. Miss Lewis, the principal of the second of these schools, was especially influential with her, and it was here that Mary Ann adopted the religious devotion and self-repression which dominated her youth.

Following the death of her mother and her sister's marriage in 1837, Mary Ann took charge of her father's household. In 1841 they moved to a house near Coventry. As she had matured Mary Ann's religious beliefs had changed, and friends whom she met here further shook her faith in Christianity. She soon decided that she could no longer attend church in good faith. Her father refused to live with her on those terms, and she went to her brother for three weeks. A reconciliation was arranged by her brother and her friends, and she agreed to resume church attendance and returned to her father. Nevertheless, her renunciation of all religious dogma was complete, and she remained agnostic until her death.

Mary Ann had continued her studies of Italian, German, Greek, and Latin. Her first published work was a translation of *Das Leben Jesu* ("The Life of Jesus") by the German theologian David Strauss. She was also contributing articles and reviews to a periodical edited by her friend Charles Bray. After the death of her father in 1849 she moved to London and became assistant editor of the *Westminster Review,* a liberal periodical. In London she met George Henry Lewes — a professional drama critic and man of letters, actor, and author of a history of philosophy — and fell in love with him. Lewes was married, but his wife had abandoned him. However, there was no chance of a legal divorce. In 1854 Lewes and Mary Ann Evans sailed together to Germany, and from that time they lived together as man and wife until his death in 1878. Their union at first made them social outcasts, but when it became apparent that this was no irresponsible affair they were accepted by their friends and society as a married couple. After Lewes' death, she married, in 1880, an old friend, the American banker J. W. Cross. Soon after, on December 22, 1880, George Eliot died.

Lewes' encouragement had much to do with George Eliot's career as a writer of fiction, beginning with publication of three stories in *Blackwood's*

Magazine. These were published together in 1858 as *Scenes of Clerical Life. Adam Bede,* published in 1859, was an immediate success. It was followed by *The Lifted Veil* in 1859 and her first great novel, *The Mill on the Floss,* in 1860. *Silas Marner* appeared in 1861. Her later works include *Romola* (1862-63); *Felix Holt* (1866); *The Spanish Gypsy* (1868), which is a drama in blank verse; a volume of verses, *The Legend of Jubal and other Poems* (1874); and a volume of essays, *The Impressions of Theophrastus Such.* The novel generally considered to be her masterpiece is *Middlemarch,* published in 1871-72.

Silas Marner, The Mill on the Floss, and *Adam Bede* form a group which make use of childhood recollections and the rural world Eliot knew in Warwickshire. She said that *Silas Marner* came to her "first of all, quite suddenly, as a sort of legendary tale suggested by my recollection of having once, in early childhood, seen a linen-weaver with a bag on his back." The novel uses other aspects of her childhood as well, including her knowledge of both Anglican worship and the more enthusiastic forms of Christianity.

However, the story was shaped in the mind of a mature and highly intelligent woman, and it represents the beliefs of her maturity. Two ideas which are expressed in Eliot's letters of about this time are that "the idea of God...is the ideal of a goodness entirely human," and that "no man can begin to mould himself on a faith or an idea without rising to a higher order of experience." Eliot believed strongly in the interdependence of men, and in all her novels she is greatly concerned to discover what might be considered good and what bad in their social relationships. *Silas Marner* is no exception. Eliot said of the book that "it sets — or is intended to set — in a strong light the remedial influences of pure, natural human relations."

BRIEF SYNOPSIS

In the village of Raveloe there lives a weaver named Silas Marner. He is viewed with distrust by the local people, for he comes from a distant part of the country. In addition he lives completely alone, and he has been known to have strange fits. For fifteen years he has lived like this.

Fifteen years earlier Silas was a respected member of a church at Lantern Yard in a city to the north. His fits were regarded there as a mark of special closeness to the Holy Spirit. He had a close friend named William Dane, and he was engaged to marry a serving-girl named Sarah. But one day the elder deacon fell ill and had to be tended day and night by members of the congregation, as he was a childless widower. During Silas' watch a bag of money disappears from a drawer by the deacon's bed. Silas' knife is found in the drawer. Silas swears he is innocent and asks that his room be searched. The empty bag is found there by William Dane. Then Silas remembers that he last used the knife to cut a strap for William; but he says nothing to the others.

In order to find out the truth the church members resort to prayer and drawing of lots, and the lots declare Silas guilty. Silas, betrayed by his friend and now by his God, declares that there is no just God. He is sure that Sarah will desert him too, and he takes refuge in his work. He soon receives word from Sarah that their engagement is ended, and a month later she marries William Dane. Soon afterward Silas leaves Lantern Yard.

He settles in Raveloe, where he feels hidden even from God. His work is at first his only solace; but soon he begins to receive gold for his cloth; and the gold gives him a kind of companionship. He works harder and harder to earn more of it and stores it in a bag beneath his floor. His contacts with humanity wither. Once he gives help to a woman who is ill by treating her with herbs as his mother taught him; but this gives him a reputation as a maker of charms. People come for miles to ask his help, and he cannot give any. As a result he is believed to cause other misfortunes and be in league with the devil. After that Silas is more alone than ever.

The greatest man of Raveloe is Squire Cass. His wife is dead, and his sons are left to their own devices. Some trouble results from this: the eldest son, Godfrey, has made a hasty marriage with a woman of poor reputation; and the second son, Dunstan, is blackmailing him to keep their father from knowing. Godfrey has given Dunstan some rent money from one of his father's tenants; now the Squire wants the money; so Godfrey gives Dunstan his horse to sell to raise the cash.

On the way to the hunt where he hopes to sell the horse, Dunstan passes the weaver's cottage. This gives him the idea of borrowing the money from Marner, but he rather likes the idea of vexing his brother, so he continues to the hunt and makes the sale. However, instead of turning over the horse at once, he rides in the chase and kills the animal on a stake.

Dunstan begins to walk home. It becomes dark and foggy before he can reach there, and in the darkness he comes to Marner's cottage. Dunstan goes there to borrow a lantern and to try to get some money out of the weaver. He finds no one there. Searching around the floor, he soon finds where the money is hidden. He replaces the bricks that had covered it and carries the money away.

Silas has poor eyesight, and on his return he finds nothing wrong until he goes to take out his money to count it. When he cannot find it he feels that once again he has been robbed by an unseen power. However, he clings to the hope that there was a human thief, and he goes off to the village inn to find the constable.

At the inn the conversation has been of ghosts, and when Silas bursts in he himself is momentarily taken for a ghost. But Silas is so worked up that it is apparent he is no ghost, and when he tells of the robbery there is immediate sympathy for him. His helplessness removes any feeling that he is connected with the devil. Some of the men set out after the constable.

The news of the robbery spreads quickly, and there is soon general agreement that the thief must have been an itinerant peddler who had been in the neighborhood, for no other stranger has been noticed, and no local person could be suspected. Dunstan's disappearance is not thought strange, for that has happened before. Godfrey is not surprised either, for he soon learns that Dunstan has killed his horse. Now he decides to tell his father of his marriage. He leads up to this by telling of his horse and of the rent money which he had given Dunstan; but he gets no farther, for his father explodes with anger. This leaves Godfrey in a worse position than ever.

Silas is now treated with some consideration by his neighbors. Dolly Winthrop, especially, visits Silas and tries to coax him into attending church, at least on Christmas. However, Silas finds no connection between local religious customs and those he knows of, and Christmas finds him at home as usual.

Christmas and New Year's are the time of special festivals in Raveloe. The most important celebration is the New Year's dance at Squire Cass's home. There Godfrey is unable to keep himself away from Nancy Lammeter, the girl he has always intended to marry. Although he knows it is wrong, and that the news of his marriage must come out soon, he determines to enjoy himself with Nancy while he can. Nancy, for her part, has wanted to marry Godfrey, but his strangeness has made her cool toward him, and when he asks her forgiveness she says only that she will be glad to see anyone reform.

Meanwhile Godfrey's wife, Molly, has become determined to revenge herself for his treatment of her, and she sets out with their child to confront him at the dance. She loses her way in the snow, and at last she fortifies herself with opium, to which she has become addicted. The opium only makes her more drowsy, and Molly sinks down in the snow. Her child slips from her arms. It is attracted to a light. The light comes from the open door of Marner's cottage, where the weaver stands unaware of the child's presence. He has been looking out to see if his money might return and has been stricken by one of his fits. When he awakes, he sees gold by his hearth and thinks his money has come back; then he discovers the gold is the hair of a child. At last he overcomes his wonder enough to realize that the child has come in out of the snow, and there outside he discovers Molly's body.

Silas takes the child and hurries to Squire Cass's house to get the doctor. His entrance causes Godfrey both fear and hope, for he recognizes the child as his own, and he has hope that he may be free at last. He goes with Doctor Kimble and finds that the woman Marner found is indeed his wife and that she is dead.

The woman is buried that week, a stranger to everyone but Godfrey. Silas feels that the child has been sent to him, and he is determined to keep it. This causes even warmer feeling for him in Raveloe, and he is given much well-meant advice. Dolly Winthrop gives him real aid with the child and offers some old clothes which belonged to her son Aaron. Godfrey is glad enough to have the child cared for. He gives money for its support, but never claims it as his own.

Silas names the child Hepzibah — Eppie for short — after his mother and little sister. He finds that, unlike his gold, Eppie makes him constantly aware of the world and of other men. He gives her his wholehearted love, and everywhere he finds kindness from the other villagers.

Sixteen years pass. Nancy and Godfrey are married. Eppie has grown into a beautiful young woman. Silas is liked and respected in Raveloe. His life with Eppie has been close and happy, and Mr. and Mrs. Cass have done much for them. Dolly Winthrop has become Eppie's godmother, and she is a close friend of Silas. The two of them have discussed his old problem at Lantern Yard and considered the great differences in religion between the two places. Now Dolly's son Aaron wishes to marry Eppie, and Eppie has agreed, if Silas can live with them. She has been told of her mother, but she knows nothing of any other father, and she cannot bear to be parted from Silas.

Godfrey and Nancy, however, are childless. Their one child died in infancy. This is a great trouble to Godfrey, who has always wanted children. At one time he wished to adopt Eppie, but Nancy refused, feeling that it would be going against Providence to adopt a child when none was given naturally. Nancy has tried to make up to Godrey in other ways, and their marriage has been happy but for that one thing. Godfrey was afraid to tell her that Eppie was his own child.

On this particular Sunday Nancy is thinking over these old problems when Godfrey comes very much upset. The Stone Pits near Marner's cottage are being drained, and Dunstan's body has been found there with Silas' gold. Godfrey is forced to tell Nancy that his brother was a thief. At the same time this convinces him that all truths come out sooner or later, and he admits that Eppie is his own child. Instead of being disgusted with him, Nancy is sorry that she refused to adopt Eppie sooner. The two of them go that night to Marner's cottage to claim Eppie.

Eppie, however, does not wish to be claimed. Both she and Silas feel that no claim of blood can outweigh their years of life together. She does not want to leave Silas nor to be rescued from her low station and the prospect of marriage to a workingman. At last Godfrey goes home bitterly disappointed. He feels that he is being punished now for his earlier weakness; but he is determined to try to do his duty at last and to do all he can for Eppie even though she has refused him.

Now that he has his gold, Silas feels able to return to Lantern Yard to try to settle the matter of the old theft. He goes there with Eppie, but they find everything changed. The chapel is gone and a factory set in its place. Only the prison is left to remind Silas that this was where he once lived. He returns home no more wise than when he set out; but he agrees with Dolly that there is reason to have faith in spite of the darkness of the past.

Eppie and Aaron are married on a fine sunny day, with the wedding at Mr. Cass's expense. The young couple come to live with Silas at his cottage, where the villagers join in agreement that Silas has been blessed through his kindness to an orphaned child.

LIST OF CHARACTERS

Silas Marner
A weaver; a pale bent man with protruding eyes and poor eyesight. He is an outcast from his original home and church and at Raveloe lives a lonely, miserly existence until his gold is stolen and a child comes to replace it.

Eppie
The daughter of Godfrey Cass by a secret marriage. She is found by

Silas in his cottage after her mother dies in the snow outside. He raises her as his own daughter.

Godfrey Cass

Eppie's father. He regrets his secret marriage and wishes to marry Nancy Lammeter; but he lacks the moral courage to try to find any solution to his problems. He prefers to wait on chance.

Nancy Lammeter

Daughter of a wealthy landowner. She combines beauty with strength of character and high principles. She wishes to marry Godfrey but will not do so until she feels he has reformed.

Dunstan Cass

Godfrey's brother. Dunstan is vain, arrogant, and deceitful and appears to have no redeeming qualities. He robs Silas and disappears with the money until his body is found in the quarry.

Squire Cass

The most important citizen of Raveloe, father of Godfrey and Dunstan. He is alternately indulgent and overly strict.

Priscilla Lammeter

Nancy's sister, a plain-looking woman but not sensitive about it. She is direct and mannish in her actions and is able to laugh freely at herself.

Mr. Lammeter

Father of Nancy and Priscilla.

Molly Farren

Godfrey's wife, once pretty but degraded by her addiction to opium.

William Dane

Silas' closest friend at Lantern Yard. He betrays Silas and marries the woman to whom Silas was engaged.

Dolly Winthrop

Wife of the wheelwright. She gives Silas aid and advice with Eppie and becomes Eppie's godmother.

Aaron

Dolly's son, who later marries Eppie.

Mr. Macey

A tailor; he is one of the most engaging inhabitants of Raveloe and a leader of opinion among the lower classes.

Mr. Snell

Landlord of the Rainbow; a peacemaker in all arguments.

Bob Lundy

The butcher. A good-natured, reticent man.

Mr. Dowlas

A farrier, or veterinary; a strong believer in his own opinions, which usually differ from those of his neighbors. He thinks of himself as a strict rationalist.

Mr. Tookey

Macey's assistant, the butt of much sarcasm from the other men.

Ben Winthrop

A wheelwright, Dolly's husband, a humorous man who enjoys the company and the drink at the Rainbow.

Jem Rodney

A poacher. At first Silas suspects him of stealing his gold because Jem had once sat too long by Silas' fire.

Solomon Macey

A locally famous fiddler, brother of the tailor.

Mr. Osgood

The uncle of Nancy and Priscilla, his sister having married Mr. Lammeter.

Mrs. Osgood

She and Nancy are very close despite being related only by marriage.

Mr. Crackenthorp

Rector of the church at Raveloe. He sets an example in eating, drinking, and dancing, as well as in religious observances.

Mrs. Crackenthorp

"A small blinking woman who fidgeted incessantly."

Dr. Kimble

An apothecary, called "doctor" by tradition, although he has no diploma. He is Godfrey's uncle and godfather.

Mrs. Kimble
Wife of the doctor and sister of Squire Cass. "Her diameter was in direct proportion" to her dignity, which is very great.

The Misses Gunn
Guests at the New Year's dance. They come from higher society and are dressed in the height of fashion.

Miss Ladbrook
A less fashionable guest at the dance.

Mr. Paston
Silas' old minister at Lantern Yard.

Sarah
The woman to whom Silas was engaged at Lantern Yard.

Bob Cass
One of Godfrey's two other brothers, in addition to Dunstan.

Jane
Nancy's serving-maid after her marriage to Godfrey.

Bryce
The acquaintance to whom Dunstan sells Godfrey's horse, Wildfire, at the hunt at Batherly.

CHAPTER SUMMARIES AND COMMENTARIES

CHAPTER 1

Summary

Once it was common in country areas to see men bent under heavy bags, weavers who had come from distant places. They were distrusted by the local people because they were not "born and bred in a visible manner." One such weaver was Silas Marner, who lived near Raveloe. His pale face and protruding eyes were fearful to small boys, and he was not much liked by their parents either, for there were rumors that Silas had strange powers. Jem Rodney had seen him standing once as stiff as a dead man; but then he recovered and walked off. Moreover, Marner had cured Sally Oates when she was sick, and "he might cure more folks if he would." All in all, it was best to be on his good side.

14

Silas had come to Raveloe fifteen years earlier from a city to the north. There in Lantern Yard he had been a faithful member of a narrow religious sect, and his first fits of unconsciousness were seen as a mark of special grace. Silas was the friend of William Dane, a friendship so close that they were called David and Jonathon. Even Silas' engagement to a young serving-woman did not seem to chill that friendship. Only once William suggested that Silas' fit was a visitation of Satan; but Silas accepted the brotherly rebuke in pained silence.

At this time the senior deacon fell ill, and members of the congregation took turns tending him. During Silas' turn the deacon died. Silas thought he appeared to have been dead for some time. Silas went to seek help and then later returned to his work. That day it was reported to him that a bag of money had been taken from the bureau by the deacon's bedside, and Silas' knife had been found there. Furthermore, the empty bag was found in Silas' room. Silas remembered then that he had last used the knife to cut a strap for William, but he said nothing.

After further deliberation the church members decided to draw lots to see whether Silas told the truth. The lots declared him guilty. At this Silas declared that there was no just God, and accused William of the theft. He expected that Sarah would desert him too, and he retreated to his loom for refuge. The next day he received word that Sarah considered their engagement ended. A month later she married William Dane, and Silas departed from Lantern Yard.

Commentary

Silas Marner is to a certain extent a historical novel — that is, the setting is a time already past when the book was written, "the days when the spinning-wheels hummed busily in the farmhouses." However, the author is being ironic in saying that the book will express a state of mind "no longer to be found," meaning the distrust of strangers, the extreme provincialism of the villagers of that time. This is intended to bring home the absurdity of some feelings which are found everywhere, although perhaps not in such extreme form.

The general introduction narrows to certain men who are particularly suspect, the wandering linen weavers. Then it is further narrowed to a concentration on one particular weaver, Silas Marner of Raveloe. Silas is seen through the eyes of the small boys of Raveloe, and the picture is a fearful one. This tends to identify the reader with the impression already given, the image held by the local folk, that Silas is an untrustworthy character. Yet the impression is kept indefinite because we have already been shown that the Raveloe view is a faulted one.

Note the image used for the weavers — "remnants of a disinherited race." Silas certainly is one such: he has been literally disinherited, driven out by his people. He is further referred to as "a dead man come to life again." This image will attain the status of a symbol through Silas' frequent fits which give him the appearance of one dead and through his long exile from humanity and his reunion through the love of a child.

Silas' unsociability is partly a result of his neighbors' distrust; partly it is a cause of it. In any case, it is this that turns even his good deeds against him. When, out of honesty, he refuses to go into the business of providing charms, it becomes accepted that he has refused out of some evil purpose.

Having explained Silas' present life, the author skips back fifteen years to show the cause of his coming to Raveloe. Where the foregoing material was an explanation as seen by Raveloe, the old life is seen from Silas' point of view. It is a revelation of his true character which counterbalances the other impression. In this way the reader is given a greater understanding than any of the characters possesses; he is able to comprehend both sides of the situation and to sympathize with all the characters.

Silas' acceptance of the doctrine of his sect and of the goodness of his friend William is utterly unquestioning. There is irony in the fact that they are referred to as David and Jonathon, for it was Jonathon who saved David from death at the hand of Saul, Jonathon's father (see I Samuel, verses 18ff.). This Jonathon, instead of saving David, betrays him. Silas' "expression of trusting simplicity" is contrasted to "the self-complacent suppression of inward triumph that lurked" in William's eyes.

Silas feels betrayed by his God because he is unable to question the validity of doctrine that drawing of lots will establish guilt. His life has been built around his church and his friend. Now these props vanish, and Silas has only his work to fall back on. His engagement was a part of his church life, and it seems only natural that it should vanish too.

CHAPTER 2

Summary

Silas' life at Raveloe is so unlike that at Lantern Yard that it seems almost a dream. The countryside is different; the church has little in common with that of his old sect; even the old Power he has trusted in seems far away here.

Work claims all of his attention until he receives his first money. Then the coins seem to offer companionship. Silas comes to look forward to the evenings, when he can take pleasure in the brightness of his gold.

From his mother Silas had learned the medicinal properties of herbs, and once he uses his knowledge to bring relief to a sick woman. For some time after that he is beset by villagers wanting charms against disease or other evils. Silas knows of no such charms; but his refusal is taken as mere ill-temper; and after that he is more alone than ever.

His work and his gold draw Silas ever farther from contact with his neighbors. Only once does anything happen to show that he has any affection left: Silas drops his old pot and he saves the pieces as a memorial of its long service. After that there is only his money and his loom, and thoughts of them when he is away from home. He forgets his herbs; his life shrinks into the compass of his room.

Commentary

Once again the author uses a general beginning, presenting the proposition that "minds that have been unhinged from their old faith and love have perhaps sought this Lethean influence of exile, in which the past becomes dreamy because its symbols have all vanished, and the present too is dreamy because it is linked with no memories." This is addressed directly to the reader. Such authorial addresses are a regular part of Eliot's technique, and they serve an important function in the novel. They are intended to guide the reader's response to the actions and characters and to channel his thoughts in the desired direction. They are rarely intrusive, for it has been evident from the first that this is a "told" story. The author makes no attempt to hide behind the scenes. This is a standard technique of Victorian fiction, and it is a useful technique when used with the skill that Eliot shows. The remarks draw the reader into the novel by connecting the fictional world with the real through the person of the author. They account for the "contemplative" air of the novel, for we are presented not only with the raw event but with the results of a long process of thought on the events.

Silas' life is set as a test of the proposition the author has presented. His old life at Lantern Yard is contrasted to the new life at Raveloe, where he feels "hidden even from the heavens." The "unquestioned doctrine," the hymns, all the old "channels of divine influences" have been closed; the symbols of the past have vanished. The present is certainly dreamy, for it takes no account of the life going on outside.

This period is the crux of Silas' life for the next fifteen years. "There was nothing that called out his love and fellowship toward the strangers he had come amongst...." The author implies that such love might have saved him: this is the meaning of the long passage on his one sympathetic contact, the time he brought herbs to ease a woman suffering from heart disease. This incident is seen from Silas' point of view, to show his reasons for refusing to aid other people who wanted charms and cures. We have already been shown that his reasons were not accepted by the community. The human contact which might have drawn Silas out finally isolates him completely. It is this lack of companionship which turns him from his work to his gold as the interest of his life. Note that he does not desire wealth. To Silas, coins are friends to enjoy.

So Silas withers. Recall from the first chapter the "bent, treadmill attitude" he assumes. He becomes almost a machine himself, certainly little better than a machine. "His life had reduced itself to the mere functions of weaving and hoarding"; it is "a mere pulsation of desire and satisfaction." That image pictures the essence of Silas' life, his heartbeat, his driving force, as a mechanical process of desiring and getting. The only sign of any human feeling left in him is his saving the bits of his ruined pot as a memorial. Yet this is a hopeful sign.

A contrast which the author emphasizes is that between the religious customs of Lantern Yard and of Raveloe. This will be elaborated in later chapters; but already it is apparent that religion here is slack. There is a church "which men gazed at lounging at their own doors in service-time." The women "seemed to be laying up a stock of linen for the life to come," as though hoarding in this life would help lay up treasure in Heaven.

Note the nature images which the author uses. These compare a man to a tree or an insect, or the natural world to human society. Such images help to define the quality of the life of a person or of the community. For example, in Raveloe even the orchards look "lazy with neglected plenty." Silas seems to weave, "like the spider, from pure impulse, without reflection." His cloth is a "brownish web." Yet "the sap of affection was not all gone" — as though affection should give sustenance as sap sustains the tree.

CHAPTERS 3–4

Summary

Raveloe lies far off from busy industries. The old-fashioned country ways still hold, although prices are high and the farmers well-off. The winter feasts are times of great merrymaking. Although the finest of these may be at Mr. Osgood's, possibly the greatest abundance is to be found at the Red House, home of Squire Cass, the greatest man of Raveloe.

The Squire's wife is long dead, and his sons have turned out rather ill. The second son, Dunstan, is "a spiteful jeering fellow"; but Godfrey, the eldest, is well thought of. However, there is talk that if he goes on as he has been, he may lose the hand of Nancy Lammeter.

These two sons of the Squire are talking together in the parlor of the Red House. Godfrey has collected some rent money from a tenant and turned it over to Dunstan. Now the Squire is threatening the tenant, and Godfrey must have the money. However, Dunstan is not inclined to repay it and says that he may have to tell the Squire that Godfrey has secretly married and now will not live with his "drunken wife." When Godfrey says that he must have the money, Dunstan suggests he sell his horse, Wildfire. There is a hunt the next day at which there may be some buyers. Godfrey does not care to go, for he is looking forward to seeing Nancy at Mrs. Osgood's birthday dance the next day; and in any case he does not want to sell his horse. However, he sees there is no other way, and at last he agrees to let Dunstan take the horse and sell it for him. With that Dunstan leaves Godfrey to ruminate on the bitterness of his life.

For years Godfrey has wooed Nancy Lammeter; but in a moment of passion he had let himself be deluded into the marriage which is a blight on his life. Now he lives in fear that the marriage will be revealed to his father, who will surely disinherit him. The worst effect would be to separate him from Nancy, whose presence is his only joy.

The next morning Dunstan sets off for the hunt. As he passes Marner's cottage by the Stone Pit, he wonders why he has never thought to "persuade the old fellow" into lending his money. He almost turns back to discuss this with Godfrey, but then his inclination to vex his brother persuades him to go on and sell the horse.

At the hunt a man named Bryce buys the horse readily. However, instead of taking the horse in at once, Dunstan decides to follow the hunt. He takes one jump too many and kills the animal on a stake.

Dunstan is unharmed, but he does not relish the embarrassment of being caught walking. Since no one has seen him fall, he leaves the horse and sets out for home. Because walking is so abnormal to him he carries his whip to keep his sense of reality. The whip is Godfrey's, but Dunstan has brought it because it makes a better show than his own.

It is becoming dark and misty as Dunstan nears Raveloe. Near the Stone Pits he again comes on Marner's cottage. He is reminded of the miser's money, and he decides to stop in and borrow a lantern and perhaps discuss this money question. He finds the cottage door open and goes in. A bit of meat is cooking over the fire, so the weaver has not gone far. Dunstan wonders whether the old man is dead. If so, no one would need his money. With that Dunstan forgets that the weaver may not be dead. He quickly discovers the money in its hiding place under the brick hearth. He replaces the bricks and carries the bags out the door, closing it behind him and stepping off into the darkness.

Commentary

The people of Raveloe hold by their own scale of values, for they have never had the opportunity to compare themselves to the rest of the world. Squire Cass is a great man because he has "a tenant or two." Antiquity included all that time beyond the memory of living persons; therefore Mr. Osgood's family is considered to be "of timeless origin." Custom is set and immovable, and anything strange is suspect. Raveloe is "aloof from the currents of industrial energy and Puritan earnestness." This is another notice of the strangeness of Silas Marner, who is a refugee from Puritan earnestness and who represents industry of a sort common then.

As in the preceding chapters, the general background serves as an introduction for specific characters. The members of the Cass family are viewed swiftly, and their particular problems are mentioned in a conversational way, as the subject of Raveloe gossip. The implied contrast between the author's view and that expressed by Raveloe gives an ironic evaluation of this family whose greatness seems to consist of "a monument in the church and tankards older than King George." This may be greatness by Raveloe's standards, but the implication is that the standards are somewhat narrow.

The scene is further narrowed to Godfrey and Dunstan. In the course of their discussion they furnish the reader with the news of Godfrey's marriage. This information gives the reader a further advantage over the inhabitants of Raveloe: it allows the author to control the reader's attitude to Godfrey from this time on, through the ironic contrast between the appearance he maintains and the truth of his situation. Eliot gives her own estimate of Godfrey's character—"natural irresolution and moral cowardice"—but she modifies it by revealing his thoughts and emotions. These show that he is at least kindhearted and uneasy in his conscience. His dilemma is presented so clearly that some sympathy is necessary.

The facts of Godfrey's marriage are never given. We know only that "it was an ugly story of low passion, delusion, and waking from delusion."

The author excuses Godfrey to a certain extent by revealing that "the delusion was partly due to a trap laid for him by Dunstan." This, along with the pain his position brings him, and later his real care for Nancy keep Godfrey from ever seeming evil. He is made to look even better by introducing him at the same time as Dunstan, for Dunstan lacks all of Godfrey's redeeming features.

Unlike his brother, Dunstan is a person with real evil in him. It is not an all-pervasive evil, but more a by-product of his arrogance. He enjoys hurting Godfrey. He takes "delight in lying, grandly independent of utility." But most of all it is simple egoism which makes Dunstan so easy to dislike. A long passage is presented entirely from his point of view, and his own thoughts are the surest way to expose his arrogance. He has little good to think of anyone but himself, whom he considers "a lucky fellow," both "daring and cunning."

Dunstan's self-esteem, however, rises from no certainty of his own worth. He takes care that he should look important because he fears the opinion of others. When he stakes Wildfire, he feels "a satisfaction at the absence of witnesses to a position which no swaggering could make enviable." He is afraid to be seen walking, for "he might meet some acquaintance in whose eyes he would cut a pitiable figure." There is an ironic contrast of the author's simple statement of Dunstan's situation and his exaggerated reaction to it: to Dunstan, walking is "a remarkable feat of bodily exertion."

When he goes to the hunt, Dunstan carries Godfrey's whip, since it gives a better appearance than his own. When he covers the name, no one can see that it is Godfrey's. Dunstan cares only for appearances. The inner reality, the covered name, is nothing to him. This is also the case with his theft of Marner's gold, Dunstan does not call it theft. He goes from the idea of borrowing to the idea that Marner may be dead. Reality escapes his consideration.

In contrast to this, Godfrey is always painfully aware of the truth of his situation, even though he keeps up a false front.

Godfrey's whip serves a double function here. Dunstan takes it because it is impressive — thus the act of taking it is an indication of his character. But the whip is closely connected with Godfrey himself, for it bears his name. It may be symbolic that this whip is of value, whereas Dunstan's own is not.

Eliot never strays far from sympathy with her characters, whatever their condition; but she is well aware of the men whose lives are a round of drink, hunts, and stagnant thoughts. One of the things said in Godfrey's favor is that he is struggling to stay above that. However, his family environment pulls him down. The importance of the family in shaping lives is recognized in the contrast between the Lammeter and Cass households, a contrast which is carried on through the book. Here the "neatness, purity, and liberal orderliness" of the Lammeters is set against the Cass household, which has "more profusion than finished excellence" in provisions and more idleness than moral strength in its sons. Even after their marriage it is Nancy who will provide the order in Godfrey's household. That is one thing that Godfrey longs for: he has dreamed that Nancy "would be his wife and would make home lovely to him, as his father's home had never been." There is a contrast, too, with Godfrey's present marriage, which offers no order, no home, and no happiness.

Some minor points should be noted for future reference. The future is foreshadowed in Dunstan's advice to Godfrey to get in Nancy's graces, as "it 'ud be saving time if Molly should happen to take a drop too much laudanum some day and make a widower of you. Miss Nancy wouldn't mind being a second, if she didn't know it." He is also ironically accurate in speaking of his luck: "...whenever I fall I'm warranted to fall on my legs." Some important symbolism is introduced in connection with Dunstan. Notice that Silas' door opens to Dunstan's touch, although it appeared to be locked. When Dunstan becomes afraid that he is lost, he feels the ground before him, for he knows there are pits in the area. Once he has taken the gold, he becomes fearful and closes the door behind him "that he might shut in the stream of light." He steps forward "into the darkness." Whatever the immediate subject, Silas' life is never far from the author's consideration, and a chance thought of Dunstan's serves as a reminder and an index of the suspicion and scorn in which Silas is held in Raveloe: Dunstan recalls that "people always said he lived on mouldy bread, on purpose to check his appetite."

Nature images continue to be used as an aid to characterization. Here Godfrey is referred to as "an uprooted tree." In context this applies to the possibility of his being disinherited, and the image lends reality to his helplessness in such a situation. But Godfrey is like an uprooted tree in other ways: his marriage has cut him off from Nancy, who is the source of "the sap of affection" in him. That marriage is compared to disease in a plant — it is "a blight on his life."

"That glorious wartime" refers to the Napoleonic wars on the continent of Europe. The war "was felt to be a peculiar favour of Providence towards the landed interest" because England was short of food and no grain could come in from the continent, which Napoleon had closed off. Therefore grain prices were high and even bad farmers prospered.

CHAPTER 5

Summary

As Dunstan leaves the cottage, Silas is no more than a hundred yards away. He feels no alarm at having left his door unlocked, for there has never been any need for a lock previously. He has been out after a piece of twine he needs for his work the next day, and now he is looking forward to his supper. That supper is a piece of meat tied to its hanger with a string and his door key, and that is the reason he failed to lock the door.

Silas comes in and warms himself by the fire. He sees nothing amiss, for his eyes are weak. It is not until he decides to count his gold before supper that he finds anything wrong. The bricks are all in place, but the hole under them is empty. At first Silas does not believe the gold is gone: he searches all over the cottage, thinking he may have hidden it elsewhere. Yet at last he must face the truth. Then Silas cries out in anguish.

Silas does not know when a thief might have come. There are no tracks. He fears that it may not have been a thief, but some unseen power which delights in tormenting him. The thought of a human thief is almost a comfort to him then, and he recalls that the poacher Jem Rodney once lingered too long by the fire when he stopped to light his pipe. Silas comes at last to the idea that the robber must be caught. He does not wish to punish anyone, but he wants his gold back. He sets off for the village to proclaim his loss so that someone can recover the stolen money.

Commentary

There is no attempt to build any suspense as to whether Silas will catch Dunstan in the cottage. This is typical of Eliot's understated plots: the robbery is an important part of the tale, but it is not used for any irrelevant sense of excitement. Instead, the author uses the incident as the source of a generalization about the human condition. In turn, this generalization becomes the source of a metaphor to make Silas' trustfulness seem natural. Like all men, Silas expects that a thing will not occur because it has not occurred before; just as "it is often observable that the older a man gets, the more difficult it is to him to retain a believing conception of his own death."

The general comment by the author tends to obscure the coincidence of Dunstan's happening along at one of the few times that Silas is not at home. This is the first of several coincidences which are often pointed out as "unrealistic." However, it is not the result of any unusual circumstances. Rather, the robbery arises strictly from what we might expect to be normal activities for these two characters. It is unexpected, but not unbelievable.

Little attention is paid to the exact details of Silas' life. We learn that he rarely has meat for supper and that twine is required in his work, but there is no concentration on the physical aspects of his life or work. Eliot stresses the psychological and moral nature of character rather than external circumstances.

Plot and symbolism are subtly combined in a single sentence which is easily overlooked — Silas' hypothetical question, "What thief would find his way to the Stone-pits on such a night as this?" The emphasis here is on the pits rather than on Silas' cottage. There may be a further connection with the image used for Silas' own fear when he discovers the robbery: "A man falling into dark water seeks a momentary footing even on sliding stones...." This is a foreshadowing of the final news of Dunstan's fate.

The stone on which Silas seeks his footing is the belief that he may only have misplaced the gold. When he finds that this cannot be true, he turns almost hopefully to the thought that a thief has come; for the only alternative is that it was "a cruel power that no hands could reach, which had delighted in making him a second time desolate." Thus the robbery is connected with the first great event which shaped Silas' present life. Silas reacts in exactly the same way — the mainstay of his emotional life is removed, and he turns to his work for support. "He turned and tottered towards his loom and got into the seat where he worked, instinctively seeking this as the strongest assurance of reality." Note the connection with the concept of the "dreaminess" of life in exile, stated in Chapter 2. It is ironic that Silas fears he is dreaming only when the dream has been stolen. That his reactions here are a result of his earlier troubles gives greater continuity and depth to Silas' character.

The author re-emphasizes that his gold has been the main thing separating Silas from contact with other men. This is stated directly — "His gold, as he hung over it and saw it grow, gathered his power of loving together into a hard isolation like its own." — but it is illustrated as well, by Silas' memory of Jem Rodney, who "had said something jestingly about the weaver's money; and he had once irritated Marner, by lingering at the fire when he called to light his pipe, instead of going about his business." Because of his gold, human contact has at last become irritating to Silas. He is at the depth of his exile: gold stands between him and friendship.

CHAPTERS 6−7

Summary

The lower classes of Raveloe are gathered at the Rainbow while their betters are attending Mrs. Osgood's birthday dance. The conversation there has begun slowly this evening, with a mild argument between the farrier and the butcher over a cow which the butcher had slaughtered the day before. The landlord settles the dispute by declaring that they are both right and both wrong. However, the ownership of the cow by Mr. Lammeter leads the landlord to ask Mr. Macey to recall when Mr. Lammeter's father first came to Raveloe. Mr. Macey, before beginning the tale, directs some jibes at his assistant, Mr. Tookey. Macey and Ben Winthrop, leader of the church choir, aim some heavy humor at Tookey for his out-of-tune singing. The landlord again decides the point by allowing that everyone is right and everyone wrong. He then directs the conversation back to the subject of Mr. Lammeter's father.

This time Macey stays on his subject, pausing now and then to admit the customary questions at the usual places. He recalls that the elder Mr. Lammeter came to Raveloe from "a bit north'ard," bringing his sheep with him. He married the sister of Mr. Osgood and settled at the Warrens. Macey, in his capacity as parish clerk, helped to marry them, and he alone noticed that during the ceremony the rector reversed the key phrases, saying, "Wilt thou have this man to thy wedded wife?" and, "Wilt thou have this woman to thy wedded husband?" Macey was worried that this would invalidate the ceremony, for he couldn't decide whether the meaning or the form was the important thing. He decided "it isn't the meanin', it's the glue." But when he questioned the rector, the rector informed him that the important thing was the register.

This story is familiar to all the hearers, and they put the correct questions to Macey. The landlord asks about the land where Mr. Lammeter settled, the Warrens. Macey says it once belonged to a London tailor who tried to make his son a country gentlemen there. After the boy died, the father died raving and left all his property to a London charity. His ghost is said to haunt the stables yet.

Mr. Dowlas, the farrier, has only scorn for ghosts, but several others pity his lack of comprehension. The landlord compromises with the argument that the ability to see ghosts is like a nose for smelling cheese: some have it and some don't.

At this moment Silas is seen standing within the room, and even the farrier is startled by the feeling that a ghost has come among them. At last the landlord asks Silas what his business is. Silas exclaims that he has been robbed. Seeing Jem Rodney there, he demands his money back. Rodney denies taking it. At last Silas is made to sit down and tell his story. In the end he apologizes to Jem for accusing him.

Silas is so distraught that there is immediate sympathy for him, and all suspicion vanishes. The farrier proposes that "two of the sensiblest o' the company" should go for the constable, who is ill in bed, and have one appointed as a deputy. The farrier clearly expects to be deputy himself. However, Mr. Macey recalls that his father told him that no doctor could be a constable, and even a cow doctor is a doctor. The farrier doesn't wish to decline the title of doctor, but argues that the law means that a doctor doesn't have to serve if he wishes not to. Nevertheless, he is driven by Macey's "merciless reasoning" to deny that he wants to be the constable. The landlord settles the dispute by persuading the farrier to go as the second man.

Commentary

The company at the Rainbow serve as a sort of chorus to comment on the action. These characters also help to round out the local society as a background for the main characters. The discussion before Silas' entry is not strictly essential to the plot, but it modifies our response to the other characters and gives wider meaning and application to the main events.

Raveloe society, which has already been commented on by the author, is now seen in the flesh. Both these and the central characters are conceived as being fully a part of the social structure. Eliot depicts character as being rooted in environment or defined within one social structure. These people cannot be uprooted: it would be hard to imagine Mr. Macey, for example, in any other surroundings. Yet there is very little description of these characters; the emphasis is on their psychology and moral nature. They are visualized through their reactions to other people and events. Their reactions are distinct enough that different characters are fully distinguished, but they fall well short of caricature.

The background of the story (and of the village) is filled in during the conversation. A good deal is said of the character of the Lammeter family, and this pertains directly to the relationship of Godfrey and Nancy. There is also a renewal of the examination of Raveloe religion. Of superstition there is plenty, but no great amount of religious thought or feeling. Christianity is semi-magical here. For example, Macey is much concerned with just which element of the ceremony makes a wedding valid.

The choosing of a deputy constable plays on the importance of ceremony by taking a mock-ceremonial form. It is based on the ritual of *nolo episcopari* — that is, the ceremony preceding the consecration of a bishop, in which the candidate formally denies any desire to become bishop.

There is little real thought of any sort exhibited. The conversation runs on in a set pattern (chorus-like) with everyone knowing his part. It is for this reason that the landlord can agree with both sides of an argument when the two cannot be logically reconciled. There is no thought involved. He is simply the peacemaker — it is in his interest to be so, and it is felt to be his proper part.

There is a third sort of ceremony mentioned, in addition to religion and conversation. This is the observance of custom. Mr. Lammeter was first respected as "a new parish'ner as know'd the rights and customs o' things, and kep a good house, and was well looked on by everybody." Custom and ceremony are the threads which hold the social fabric together. By observing them, Mr. Lammeter was quickly accepted, even though, like Silas, he came from "a bit north'ard." That Silas partakes neither of the ceremony of the church nor the public house is a contribution to his exiled state.

Silas' appearance is suited to the conversation which has been taking place. Recall that in the first pages of the novel the Raveloe people referred to him as "a dead man come to life again." His appearance now is like that in those fits which led to his reputation: he appears as if "his soul went loose from his body." In a figurative sense this is true, for Silas' whole life was centered in his gold, which is now gone from him. It is this that causes his deathly appearance.

The excellent humor of the debate over who shall be constable is based on a multiple development of irony. First there is irony of action — that is, events turn out the opposite of what was intended. The farrier confidently volunteers as a deputy, but in the end professional pride forces him to declare that he does not want to go. Along with this is an irony of statement: the implied meaning of the words is the opposite of their face value. Thus when the author speaks of the farrier's "pregnant speech," she means the speech was dull and empty. A third sort of irony rises from the difference between the author's implied view of a situation and that stated by a character. Macey wonders at his own "'cuteness," while his reasoning is actually based on a twisted logic; and the farrier is persuaded to go for the constable as "a second person disinclined to act officially," although his inclination to act officially is very great indeed.

This debate, like the earlier conversation among the company, contains some fine comic dialogue. It offers some good examples of Eliot's ability to fit comedy to a variety of characters without lapsing into farce.

Summary

When Godfrey comes home that night, he is too preoccupied with Nancy Lammeter to be surprised that Dunstan has not come home. The next morning he is as busy as the rest of the village in discussing the robbery.

The rain has washed away all footprints near the cottage, so the only evidence is a tinderbox which was found there. A minority of the villagers feel that this is not a robbery that can be solved by human powers anyway; but Mr. Snell, the landlord of the Rainbow, recalls that about a month before a peddler had been in Raveloe and he had carried a tinderbox. This recollection leads other people to remember the man. It is recalled that he had rings in his ears and was altogether a suspicious person. Silas remembers only that the man came to his door and went away at once; but it is remarked that a "blind creatur" like Silas would hardly have noticed the man lurking in the hedgerows.

There is no attempt to link Dunstan's disappearance to the robbery, for Dunstan has gone off before for long periods. However, Godfrey is anxious about his horse, and he sets off to Batherly to look for Dunstan. On the way he meets Bryce, who was to have bought the horse. Bryce tells him that Dunstan has killed Wildfire, but he does not know where Dunstan has gone.

Godfrey begins to fear that when Dunstan returns he will tell the whole story rather than bear their father's anger alone. Godfrey decides that to forestall this he must admit the truth himself. All that day he manages to maintain a resolve to make a complete avowal in the morning; but waking in the night he can only feel that if Dunstan does not come back for a few days, everything may blow over.

In the morning at breakfast Godrey opens the subject with the news that Dunstan has staked Wildfire. He says that now he will be unable to pay the Squire the hundred pounds which the tenant Fowler has paid him for rent. The Squire goes purple with anger on finding that Godfrey has given the money to Dunstan. He demands that Dunstan be brought in to account for it. When he learns that Dunstan has not come back, he wants to know why Godfrey gave him the money in the first place. At this Godfrey hesitates and finally says that it was only a bit of foolery between him and Dunstan. Squire Cass insists that it is time Godfrey had done with fooleries. He asks why Godfrey hasn't married Lammeter's daughter as he once seemed to intend and offers to ask her for him, if Godfrey hasn't the courage.

Godfrey says uncomfortably that he would rather manage for himself and hopes that his father won't say anything. His father intends to do as he chooses, and he instructs Godfrey to tell Dunstan that he need not come home again.

Godfrey is left more entangled than ever. He falls back on the hope that chance may favor him in the future.

Commentary

The scene shifts from Silas to Godfrey at the same time that the news of the robbery spreads from the group present at the Rainbow to the upper part of Raveloe society. A "higher consultation" is carried out under Mr. Crackenthorp, "assisted by Squire Cass and other substantial parishioners." Thus the portion of the plot involving Silas and that centered on Godfrey begin to be brought together through the "background" characters.

It is not surprising that no one suspects Dunstan of the robbery. Despite his bad character, he is above suspicion as a member of the leading family of the village. In any case, no local person would be suspected if an outsider is available. This is exactly the sort of mistrust that Silas himself has faced. Eliot shows that it is unreasoning mistrust: a peddler is suspected because "men of that sort, with rings in their ears, had been known for murderers often and often; there had been one tried at the 'sizes not so long ago but what there were people living who remembered it."

This is not really very often, but it is often enough for people who believe that "everybody had a right to their own opinions, grounds or no grounds." In Raveloe, reputation for veracity is based on external evidences of character. The virtues are felt to be all of a piece. Hence the glazier's wife, "whose house was among the cleanest in the village," is thought to be certainly truthful. The author herself shows some belief in this in her treatment of the Lammeters, whose excellence extends to both morality and housekeeping, and the Casses, whose laxness carries over from the home to moral principle. However, the events demonstrate that this system is not valid for people whose imaginations overreach their sense of abstract "truth." Silas, being both honest and unimaginative, can recall nothing suspicious of the peddler, even though he "clutched strongly at the idea of the pedlar's being the culprit." But others, including the glazier's wife, can easily recall whatever seems to be required by the case.

Godfrey is placed a cut above the other characters by his refusal to become excited about the peddler. His levelheadedness, however, is coupled with that weakness of will already noted. The author restates her opinions of Godfrey here. He is annoyed at his father's obduracy, but "he was not critical on the faulty indulgence which preceded these fits; *that* seemed to him natural enough." Indulgence to Eliot is as much a fault as is lack of sympathy, and she tries to guide the reader, too, into that conviction.

To aid in this, she presents a scene between Godfrey and Squire Cass as a specific examination of the laxness of the Cass household. Note the particular point that "every one breakfasted at a different hour in the Red House." There is no ceremony here, no family ritual. The Squire himself shows "marks of habitual neglect, his dress was slovenly." Slovenliness, through constant connection with weakness and indulgence, comes to represent both cause and symbol of the moral weakness of the family. In this case it leads into an example of Godfrey's irresolution at the crisis—his failure to tell his father of his marriage.

Eliot uses this event as the focus of a general statement to the reader. Like most such statements in the book, this is a gloss on an idea which is also integrated into the structure of the novel. What Eliot says here about Chance is also brought out in action in the story.

In this one scene Squire Cass takes on his full character. This is done almost entirely through his conversation, added to the author's personal comments. What description there is of him is brief and general. His talk gives him a strongly marked personality, but he is not developed in depth. The Squire serves conveniently as the hammer which Godfrey fears will crush him on the anvil of his marriage.

Note the metaphor of religion for chance. This is a further expression of the author's examination of religion of all sorts. Godfrey does indeed worship Chance. He has only fear for "orderly sequence," for that must lead to the discovery of his marriage. Chance is good to Godfrey now; yet it is the orderly sequence which triumphs in the end. It is this "orderly sequence by which the seed brings forth a crop after its kind" which had developed Godfrey's moral laxity from his father's indulgence. The seed of his present irresolution brings forth a crop which will haunt his future life.

CHAPTER 10

Summary

Raveloe opinion on the robbery continues to be divided between the idea that the peddler was the thief and the theory that this is an impenetrable mystery. But while his neighbors argue, Silas is baffled and desolate. However, there is a kindlier feeling toward him now, and he receives visits from well-meaning neighbors. Mr. Macey comes to advise Silas to acquire a Sunday suit and go to church. Dolly Winthrop comes on much the same mission. She is a "good, wholesome woman" who is always there when help is needed, and now she comes with her little son Aaron to bring Silas a gift of cakes. On the cakes she has pricked the letters I.H.S., in imitation of the church pulpit-cloth. She does not know their meaning, but she feels they may have some good effect. Dolly remarks that Silas does not attend church, and he replies that he has never been to church, although he used to attend chapel. This is beyond Dolly's comprehension, but she urges him at least to give up weaving on Sundays.

Nevertheless, Christmas day finds Silas alone as always, while in the village the bells ring and the church is full. After church there are feasts and parties. These are family parties, but they look forward to the great dance at the Red House on New Year's Eve.

Godfrey, too, looks forward to the dance as a chance to see Nancy, but he fears that Dunstan may return or that his father will bring matters to a head.

Commentary

Justice Malam "could draw much wider conclusions without evidence than could be expected of his neighbours." This is the ironic summing up of the Raveloe attitude to the robbery, or to mysteries in general. The little thought which exists is devoted to fancies. However, these fancies lead to a kindlier feeling toward Silas, even though it is mixed with a good deal of self-interest and complacency. Mr. Macey can be insulting while trying to be complimentary: "it isn't every queer-looksed thing as Old Harry's had the making of — I mean, speaking o' toads and such; for they're often harmless, like, and useful against varmin. And it's pretty much the same wi' you, as fur as I can see." But he is at least trying to be helpful, and if he gives advice, he believes it to be the best obtainable.

Not all the help Silas receives is of that type, either. Dolly Winthrop is one person who is thoughtful as well as sincere. The essence of Dolly's personality is that she is a "good, wholesome woman." She represents the good part of humanity, the possibility of real concern with the problems of other people. But she is more than mere representation: as the story progresses, she acquires enough of a personality and a background to take on the qualities of a real person. (Compare her to Macey, who is more limited in his reactions. Macey always presents a single simple reaction to every situation—but he does so with such energy and self-certainty that he is responsible for some of the best comedy in the book.)

Silas has changed since the robbery. The change is pronounced, but it is a natural result of his misfortunes. Its roots go back all the way to the day he came to Raveloe. Note that although his condition now is almost the same as at the time of his arrival, he does not have the determination to begin again in the same way. He did not then *require* the companionship of his gold, but now he cannot be content without it and cannot set out to earn a new hoard. He has become dependent on its presence, which "fenced him in from the wide, cheerless unknown.... But now the fence was broken down—the support was snatched away." He has "no phantasm of delight to still the poor soul's craving." Yet he still has the craving—his soul is intact. And the gold was only a "phantasm" of delight—it brought no real fulfillment. Its disappearance leaves only a blank, but it prepares him for the possibility of human contacts. Already Silas is more receptive to friendly overtures; he no longer wishes that visitors would go on their way, as he once did with Jem Rodney. (Note too the symbol of the open door: "he opened the door wide to admit Dolly.")

Both Macey and Dolly urge Silas to attend church, but the long span of years since Silas left his church and his inability to understand their religion blunt their good intentions. Silas has forgotten time and the world. He has no idea how long he has been at Raveloe, and Macey doubts that he knows when it is Sunday. Silas tells Dolly he has heard the Sunday bells, but to him they have no real meaning, for "there had been no bells in Lantern Yard." Nor does he recognize Aaron's carol as religious music. The Raveloe idea of church is foreign to him, and he has no desire to return to the old ways.

We are again reminded that Raveloe religion is mostly concerned with form. Churchgoing is a good thing, but "to go to church every Sunday in the calendar would have shown a greedy desire to stand well with Heaven and get an undue advantage...." Church is only a customary part of life and not a serious business of salvation as it once was to Silas. Christmas brings with it a special service and the "Christian freedom" to eat, drink, and be merry. The service brings a vague sense of well-being which is generally beneficial and partly magical, being the result of special hymn and anthem and the Athanasian Creed, which was "of exceptional virtue, since it was only read on rare occasions."

Note the skill with which the author makes the transition from Silas' problems to Godfrey's: Dolly's remarks on religion and Christmas lead to the Christmas service, on to the family parties, and thence to the great party at the Red House on New Year's Eve.

CHAPTER 11

Summary

Nancy Lammeter, having made it clear to Godfrey Cass that she will not marry him, is quite pained to be met by him at the door when she comes to the Red House for the dance. When Squire Cass comes out to greet her father, she escapes to the bedroom where ladies are changing into their gowns. Nancy greets her aunt, Mrs. Osgood, and is introduced to the two Miss Gunns, daughters of a wine merchant from a neighboring town. The Miss Gunns, although they themselves frequent a higher society, are very taken with the beauty and natural charm of Nancy Lammeter. They think it a pity, however, that her hands should be coarse from housework and that her speech show traces of rustic dialect.

Nancy's sister Priscilla enters as Nancy is changing. Priscilla and Nancy dress alike through Nancy's insistence, although Priscilla is plain-looking and unsuited to Nancy's styles. She is resigned to spinsterhood, however, and she is cheerful about the matter. Her directness is unsettling to the Miss Gunns, who are also plain but are less inclined to be told so.

At dinner Nancy is seated between Godfrey and the rector, Mr. Crackenthorp, while Priscilla accompanies her father. The rector's remarks on Nancy's beauty are an embarrassment to Godfrey, and furthermore they provoke sallies from Squire Cass and Dr. Kimble on the same subject. Godfrey fears that these may lead to an uncomfortable end.

Solomon Macey, the fiddler, soon arrives and leads the company into the parlor to open the dancing. A few of the more privileged villagers are allowed in as spectators as the dance is led off by the Squire with Mrs. Crackenthorp and the rector with Mrs. Osgood. Godfrey soon joins in with Nancy, but they quickly leave the dance again. Although the spectators assume there are romantic reasons, the truth is that Nancy has torn some stitches in her dress and is in need of repairs. The two of them wait in a side parlor for Priscilla to come. Against his intentions Godfrey is led to ask Nancy to forgive his past coldness and declares that one dance with her matters more to him than all the world. Priscilla's entrance ends the conversation.

Commentary

Eliot opens this chapter, like several preceding ones, with a general statement followed by an example. Previously the method has been used to put across points important to the meaning of the novel. Here it has a lighter purpose, the introduction of Nancy Lammeter.

Nancy is certainly as beautiful as Godfrey's musings have indicated. The point is reinforced by showing how the Miss Gunns react to her. The Miss Gunns are strangers, rather plain young women but members of a more fashionable set. They are the sort of people who have no reason to admire Nancy and every reason not to. Therefore their pleasure in her leaves the reader with the certainty that Nancy is charming as well as beautiful. The Miss Gunns can see nothing to criticize except her hands, "which bore the traces of butter-making, cheese-crushing, and even still coarser work." They pity her ignorance, for she says "'appen" for "perhaps," and "oss" for "horse." They themselves, it is noted with fine irony, "habitually said 'orse, even in domestic privacy and only said 'appen on the right occasions." Thus the Miss Gunns themselves judge by a standard which author and reader find crude. But Eliot displays sympathy and understanding once again: she addresses the reader directly to point out that while Nancy is uneducated, "yet she had the essential attributes of a lady —high veracity, delicate honour in her dealings, deference to others, and refined personal habits—and lest these should not suffice to convince grammatical fair ones that her feelings can at all resemble theirs, I will add that she was slightly proud and exacting, and as constant in her affection towards a baseless opinion as towards an erring lover." This last bit of irony is aimed directly at the reader and serves once again to bring the reader's world into that of the book.

There is considerable complexity to Nancy's character. At the moment her attitude toward her erring lover is of prime importance. She does not know how badly Godfrey has erred, but she has clearly convinced herself that he has erred too greatly to be attractive to her. It is equally clear that he *is* still attractive to her. Nancy here shows the sentiment natural to a young woman, a tendency to dramatize her emotions. She "declared to herself that not the most dazzling rank should induce her to marry a man whose conduct showed him careless of his character." Yet this dramatization does not hide the core of real principle which she has in herself and expects in others. The strength of principle will last when her youthful sentimentality has gone or mellowed into mature understanding.

Now that they are seen together, Godfrey is set in strong contrast to Nancy. He has no self-restraint. He struggles with himself, but in the end he gives up the struggle, falling back on his old determination "to get as much of this joy as he could tonight, and think nothing of the morrow."

Priscilla Lammeter shows more self-awareness and less selfishness than any other character. Priscilla is strongly characterized. As with Macey and Squire Cass, this is done mainly through her speech. Yet she is not at all like them. Where Macey's "humor" is almost always at the expense of someone else, Priscilla is cheerfully blunt at her own expense. When she is ready for the dance she claims to be "as ready as a mawkin *can* be — there's nothing a-wanting to frighten the crows, now I've got my ear-droppers in." Priscilla knows herself in a way that Nancy does not: she knows she is unlikely to marry and has prepared herself to live with her father. In contrast, Nancy talks of not intending to marry, and thinks she means it; but it is evident that she is the sort of woman who must marry, and no sentimental vow will help her. Priscilla's humor conceals a seriousness deeper than the outer seriousness Nancy displays.

The gathering at the Red House is the upper-class equivalent of the company at the Rainbow. It forms a second chorus which continues to fill in the background of life in Raveloe and to comment on the action. In this case the comment is mostly on the second main plot division, the romance of Godfrey and Nancy. The talk again follows a traditional pattern, with "safe, well-tested personalities" providing the humor for the company. There is no great difference between the "high society" seen here and the "low society" of the Rainbow; and even such differences as exist are partly submerged when the dancing begins and the villagers are let in as spectators. This provides a cross-current of comment in which lower-class opinion is freely given on the doings of the great, and especially on Nancy and Godfrey.

A sort of community point of view is used to give the villagers' ideas about this festivity. Their ideas reflect the desirability of custom and ceremony. It is felt to be a social duty "to be merry at appropriate times" and pay each other "old-established compliments in sound traditional phrases." Custom is rigorously followed. Squire Cass leads off the dance, "and the charter of Raveloe seemed to be renewed by the ceremony." Custom and ceremony, like religion, maintain the stability of society by renewing the old traditions and truths. The dance at the Red House is analogous to the Christmas religious service — it brings a sense of well-being in the community, as the latter brought a sense of personal well-being.

Notice should be taken of the ironic statement that Nancy's thoughts were "much occupied with love struggles, but hardly so as to be insensible to a disorder in the general framework of things." The disorder referred to is in the stitches of Nancy's dress; but she is certainly insensible to the nature of the disorder in Godfrey's life. His broken marriage is truly a disorder "in the general framework of things." The reference may be carried a step further, to the disorder which Silas feels in the whole framework of a world which has betrayed him. Note too the next statement, an indication perhaps of Nancy's attitude of life: "Nancy...completed her duty in the figure they were dancing...." This restates the contrast between Nancy and Godfrey, her partner in the figure—Nancy is always careful to do her duty. If she is not always sensible of disorder, she is careful not to create any.

CHAPTER 12

Summary

While Godfrey and Nancy are dancing, Godfrey's wife Molly is walking through the snow toward Raveloe carrying her child in her arms. Her addiction to opium, far more than her husband's neglect, is the cause of her present ragged drabness. Nevertheless, she intends to revenge herself on Godfrey by appearing at the dance and revealing that she is his wife. Molly started out early, but the snow has held her back, and now she becomes too tired to go on. To comfort her she takes the last remnant of her opium. This only increases her weakness, and at last she sinks down in the snow in a stupor.

The child slips down into the snow. It discovers a bright light coming across the night and toddles toward it. The light comes from the open door of the weaver's cottage, where Silas stands unconscious in one of his fits. He has been told that to watch the new year in is good luck and may bring his money back, and he has been watching out the door for some sign of the gold.

When Silas recovers, he thinks for a moment that his gold *has* come back, for on the hearth he sees a blurred vision of a heap of coins. When he touches them, he finds they are the golden hair of a sleeping child. The surprise brings him the memory of his little sister and of Lantern Yard. Then the child wakes. It cries because its shoes are wet, and this leads Silas at last to the body outside in the snow.

Commentary

This cold miserable scene follows immediately on the gay warmth of the party, giving a striking contrast between the two sides of Godfrey's life. But once the point is made, the effect is softened. Up to now Godfrey has looked bad because his marriage has never been fully explained. The reason for it is still not given, but a look at his wife makes Godrey's rejection of her seem more reasonable. The author withdraws sympathy from Molly by making her degradation her own responsibility and by assigning her only the worst traits of character. "Molly knew that the cause of her dingy rags was not her husband's neglect but the demon Opium to whom she was enslaved...." She sets out for Raveloe as "a premeditated act of vengeance," but "her indolence" leads her to linger on the road, and even her "vindictive purpose" cannot keep her moving in the snow. By these means the author keeps in the background a death which could be made heartrending in other circumstances.

By coincidence Molly arrives at her death just beyond Silas' door at a time when that door stands open. This is a coincidence less believable than that by which Dunstan arrived during Silas' absence. Still it is not beyond possibility, and the action is presented in such a way that the problem is glossed over. The child sees a light and goes to it; the light comes from Silas' door; the reason that the door is open is given; and the problem of the child's being just outside the door in the first place is forgotten.

In any case, not too much weight should be put on the physical details of the incident. The events should be judged not by the way they reflect ordinary experience, but by their cohesiveness and meaning within the total context of the story. In this case events may be taken both literally and as symbols of human experience. Silas' open door is symbolic of his readiness for human contact. Still, there is a logical reason for it—he has taken to standing at his door looking out on the chance that his gold may be returned. Tonight he is up because he has been told that "he must sit up and hear the old year rung out and the new rung in, because that was good luck." This is Silas' first acceptance of local custom, a further sign of his willingness to re-enter society. It also functions as the physical cause of his unusual excitement which leads to one of his fits.

Silas turns back into his cottage "unaware of the chasm in his consciousness." We may recall that the loss of his gold created a "blank filled with grief," while Silas remained unaware of the real "chasm," the need for human contacts. Now Silas is prepared for the return of his gold, and for a moment he thinks it *has* come back. There is no transfer of his love yet. He mistakes the child's hair for real gold. Even after he recognizes the reality, the gold image clings ("soft yellow rings all over its head") as though his mind clung still to the past.

It is interesting to note some of the parallels which have developed in the plot: a robbery first sent Silas to Raveloe and closed his heart against men. Now a robbery leads him to open his door to mankind; but the door admits (without his knowledge) the child who is to reopen his heart. Silas' next reaction is the same as at the time of the robbery—he mistrusts his senses, thinking that this is a dream. This is still another means of connecting the child with the gold. Finally Silas thinks this may be his little sister brought back to him. This brings to him memories of Lantern Yard. This is the first memory of his old life since he left it. He feels that "this child was somehow a message come to him from that far-off life." Silas' present life is finally being united with his past.

CHAPTER 13

Summary

To avoid his father's pointed jokes, Godfrey is standing off from Nancy while still staying where he can watch her. He is startled by the sudden entrance of Silas Marner carrying his own child. Silas asks for the doctor to go to the woman near his cottage. At this Godfrey feels only fear that the woman may not be dead. The women ask whose the child is. Silas cannot say. But when Mrs. Kimble suggests that he leave it there, Silas refuses to part with it.

Godfrey goes for Dolly Winthrop and they follow the doctor to the Stone Pits. He waits until Dr. Kimble comes out with the news that the woman is dead. Then he goes in to have a last look at his wife. He feels a twinge of jealousy at the contentment the child shows in Silas' arms. When he asks if Silas will take the child to the parish to be raised, Silas answers that the child has come to him and he will keep it. Godfrey gives him money and returns home with a sense of relief.

Commentary

Silas' entry at the Red House parallels the earlier one at the Rainbow. It is seen from the point of view of the spectators: Silas is not seen approaching, but appears suddenly amid the festivities. Once again there is the feeling that a ghost has burst in, but this time only Godfrey feels it, and he is looking at the child. Eliot continues her careful handling of Godfrey. Even when he pretends not to know his child and his dead wife, he seems not evil but weak. He is "half-smothered by passionate desire and dread," yet he has the sense that "he ought to accept the consequences of his deeds, own the miserable wife, and fulfil the claims of the helpless child. But he had not moral courage enough to contemplate that active renunciation of Nancy as possible for him; he had only conscience and heart enough to make him forever uneasy under the weakness...."

Godfrey is kept from seeming wicked, but we are never allowed to forget the consequences of his weakness—what it has done to him as well as to others. When he first hears of the woman's death, his first emotion is the "evil terror" that she might not be dead. Yet he feels regret that the child seems happy with Marner and shows no response to his own "half-jealous yearning."

At the moment it would appear that Godfrey's weakness has been rewarded, that all is well with him. But there are hints that things are not concluded yet. One is Godfrey's jealousy about the child. Another is that Godfrey is uneasy about his wrongdoing. And his weakness is not ended: he desires to help the child, but he does not dare to admit it is his. "As for the child, he would see that it was cared for—he would never forsake it; he would do everything but own it." The strongest implication that all is not settled for Godfrey comes as he looks at his dead wife, in the statement that "at the end of sixteen years every line in the worn face was present to him when he told the full story of this night."

Silas' actions are in strong contrast to Godfrey's. He has no knowledge of the child except that it has come to him in place of his gold, but he is determined to keep it. He makes no vows to himself, but he *acts,* as Godfrey does not—in effect he "owns" the child. This reaction is "almost like a revelation to himself," for he had no such intention a minute before. Despite the rational explanation, then, the child's coming seems a miracle of sorts. But if the event and the change seem miraculous to Silas and the other characters, they are no miracles to the reader, who has been carefully prepared for them.

CHAPTERS 14—15

Summary

Molly is buried that week, but hardly anyone notices. The villagers are surprised at Silas' determination to keep the child, but it leads to greater sympathy for him, and he receives much advice on child-raising. The most acceptable help comes from Dolly Winthrop, who gives Silas some of Aaron's old clothes and shows him how to dress and bathe the child. She also suggests that if Silas wishes to do the right thing by the child, she must be christened at church. Silas doesn't understand the word, but after Dolly explains it to him he decides the child should be named Hepzibah after his mother and his little sister. She is to be called Eppie for short.

As time passes the child creates new links with the world for Silas. His gold had always kept his thoughts inward, but Eppie leads them out into the world like a reawakening to life. Eppie soon develops a capacity for mischief, and Silas is troubled about having to punish her. He cannot bear to spank her, so he takes Dolly's advice to try shutting her in the coal hole. He tries this only once, after Eppie has run away into a neighboring field. Eppie finds the coal hole as much fun as the fields, and Silas drops all idea of punishing her in the future. Silas takes her on his trips to the farmhouses, and Eppie makes him seem human to his neighbors. Even the children no longer fear him. And now that he has the child, the gold he earns seems unimportant.

Godfrey watches the weaver's growing happiness with hidden interest. He dares not claim the child as his own, and he sees that she is well taken care of. Godfrey has no regrets now. Dunstan has not returned; Godfrey's courtship of Nancy is going well; he envisions himself happily married, playing with his children on his own hearth.

Commentary

Molly's burial, like her death, is told but not seen. Her passing creates no stir in the world portrayed in the novel, and it is not allowed to disturb the reader. Silas and the child remain the focus of attention.

The time of this section stretches from the burial to some indeterminate point apparently several years later. In its course the full nature of the miracle becomes apparent. The author now gives a central statement of that which has been shown—that the child represents the beginning of human contacts for Silas: "...as the weeks grew to months, the child created fresh and fresh links between his life and the lives from which he had hitherto shrunk continually into narrower isolation." From the beginning Silas has felt this miraculous nature of the child. He tells Dolly, "Yes—the door was open. The money's gone I don't know where, and this is come from I don't know where." Now the child causes love to grow within him, and at the same time he finds love, or at least friendliness, among other men. Note particularly that "no child was afraid of approaching Silas when Eppie was near him." Recall that when Silas was first seen his gaze was enough to make "small scoundrels...take to their legs in terror." His outlook has changed, and so has theirs.

There is further notice taken that Eppie helps Silas to remember the past he had forgotten. Once again there is the connection with his little sister, for she had the same name. Then, too, he begins to go out, to notice the world again, and he remembers "the once familiar herbs...with their unchanged outline and markings...." Before his flight to Raveloe, Silas felt that the world was changed. Now he finds that it is still the same, but that *he* had changed.

Eppie is a treasure of a different sort from gold. It is ironic that Dolly recommends she be punished, if necessary, by being put in the coal hole; for though this is a punishment for Eppie, it is what Silas did daily to his gold. Also, "the gold had asked that he should sit weaving longer and longer, deafened and blinded more and more to all things...but Eppie called him away from his weaving and made him think all its pauses a holiday...." His life had all been drawn inward on itself; now it is directed out into the world.

For the most part Silas' contacts with other persons now are narrated rather than shown. The only person who is treated dramatically is Dolly. There are several possible reasons for this. It allows the building of one meaningful relationship for Silas rather than several haphazard ones. This in turn leads to a fuller treatment of other problems later on — among them Silas' past and Eppie's future. Besides, Dolly as a representative of the best in human character is a counterbalance to some others. Eliot gives one particular example to show the goodness of Dolly Winthrop: she brings Eppie some clothes, but insists that Silas dress her so that "you can say as you've done for her from the first of her coming to you."

Dolly is not exceptionally bright, however. Intellectually she may be taken to represent the average of Raveloe folk. This gives her comments added value for the purposes of explaining Raveloe life. One of particular interest is her belief that Eppie should be christened. "For if the child ever went anyways wrong, and you hadn't done your part by it, Master Marner — 'noculation, and everything to save it from harm — it 'ud be a thorn i' your bed forever...." Religion is a spiritual equivalent of vaccination, a charm to ward off ill results.

Hepzibah, as Silas says, is a Biblical name. Appropriately, it means "my delight is in her." This is an allusion to Isaiah 62:4 — "Thou shalt no more be termed forsaken...but thou shalt be called Hepzibah...for the Lord delighteth in thee."

Godfrey now "seemed like a man of firmness." But the author is being ironic. Godfrey "seemed" firm, to those who do not know the truth. And there are other shadows of the future. He pictures himself happy at home with Nancy and his children, and he intends to provide for the other child because "that was a father's duty." He still does not recall that it is his duty to own the child. The author brings in the metaphor of the ring that "pricked its owner when he forgot duty and followed desire." She remarks that it may not have pricked deeply "when he set out on the chase," but become painful only when "hope, folding her wings, looked backward and became regret." The implication is that although Godfrey has not been hurt yet, he still may be, and it will have something to do with his child. This is typical of Eliot's careful preparation for future events, so that they do not seem strange or unreal when they come.

CHAPTER 16

Summary

It is sixteen years since Silas found his new treasure. The church bells are ringing as the villagers come from church. Among the crowd are Godfrey Cass, looking much the same as the young man of twenty-six, and his wife Nancy, who is still lovely but "ripened into fuller goodness." Also to be seen are Silas and his daughter, a blonde girl of eighteen. With them is Aaron Winthrop. Eppie is suggesting to her father, Silas, that they might have a garden, and Aaron eagerly offers to help plant it. Silas is willing, and he asks that Aaron's mother be consulted, as she is always ready with good advice.

At their home Silas and Eppie are greeted by various animals — donkey, dog, and tortoise-shell kitten. The animals are not the only additions to the cottage since Eppie arrived. Furniture has been provided by Mr. Cass, and the home is quite comfortable. On the advice of the local sages Silas has taken up smoking a pipe for his health. This is only part of the new self which has developed since Eppie came. He has discussed with Dolly the old robbery at Lantern Yard, and they have puzzled over the differing customs of the two places. Dolly cannot believe there is another person so bad as William Dane, and after much rumination of the tale she concludes that Silas should have trusted that a higher being would have made things right, for if he had gone on trusting his old friends he would never have run away and been so alone. Silas, now that Eppie has been sent to him, agrees in part; but to him the drawing of the lots is still dark.

This conversation took place in Eppie's early years. Since then she and Silas have lived in perfect love and mutual happiness. Eppie has been told of her mother, as much as is known. Of her real father she knows nothing. Now that the garden is planned, however, Eppie decides that she would like the furze bush where her mother's body was found moved into the garden. Silas agrees to this, but he is worried about carrying stones for a wall. Eppie is sure there will be plenty of stones, for the Stone Pits are being drained by Mr. Godfrey Cass, who has taken over that land. As for carrying them, Aaron will do that. Eppie is sure of that, for Aaron has asked her to marry him. Eppie has told him, however, that Silas must live with them, for she will never leave him alone. Silas feels that she is young for marriage, but if she wishes it he will not object. He asks that they consult Dolly on the matter.

Commentary

This section of the book opens in the present tense. This helps the reader to adjust to the sixteen-year gap in time by giving an immediacy to the action, as though what has gone before were in the past and this is what is happening *now*. After a few paragraphs the author drops back into the the past tense to continue the story.

The changes that have taken place in the main characters are quickly filled in. Godfrey has changed not at all, except that he looks older. Nancy, however, has matured in more than years. Her soul has grown into "fuller goodness." Something of the same sort has happened to Silas. We learn that "his large brown eyes seem to have gathered a longer vision, as is the way with eyes that have been short-sighted in early life...." This is a physical change, to be sure; but it is more than that. His eyes were "short-sighted" in more than a physical sense, and he has been helped to overcome that.

The events of the intervening years are also filled in in a few brief lines. Part of this occurs in conversations. Aaron says that Mr. Cass would be willing to give Silas and Eppie some soil for a garden. Thus we know that Godfrey has to some extent honored his vow to provide for Eppie. Silas and Eppie want Dolly to know all about the garden; so it is certain that she has continued in her kindness to them. Later we see that she is Eppie's godmother. The first exchange of conversation also establishes that more than friendship exists between Eppie and Aaron. In this way a lot of important background is got out of the way quickly.

Silas' position in the community is seen to be firmly established now. Through his kindness to Eppie he has come to be regarded as "an exceptional person"; and Eppie has brought him fully into line with the community. He is now a churchgoer; he has taken up a pipe on the advice of "the sages of Raveloe"; he is friendly with his neighbors. His present is well-grounded in happiness, and there is even a hint that he may be in for a larger reward — Macey at least is certain that what Silas had done "was a sign that his money would come to light again." Furthermore, Silas, through pondering over his old faith, has "recovered a consciousness of unity between his past and his present." The author states this directly, but she has already shown it through his memories of Lantern Yard and of his herb medicine. All three phases of Silas' life have been united. Yet there still remains for Silas one problem — that of settling the truth of the first robbery. His conversations with Dolly show that this bothers him.

Consideration of this problem leads to a new depth of character for Dolly. Throughout the book we have seen that character is closely linked to structure: Silas has developed with the changing situation. Here Dolly develops in the same way, or at least the reader's impression of her changes. She is ignorant, but she has great inner resources, and these are gradually revealed. She has to struggle against "narrow outward experience" which "gave her no key to strange customs." This, in fact, is exactly the problem which the author is at pains to overcome in the reader, by giving full inward and outward information about many characters. Dolly is not given that information, but she has a wide inward experience, at least. She has a sympathy broad enough to include even those who have harmed her friend.

Dolly's advice to "trusten" may seem naive in the face of the real evils which have occurred in Silas' life. It is not easy to tell just what the author's belief is on this point. Yet it is certain that Silas has come to see good in his fellow men. Partly this is semi-superstitious, a belief that Eppie was sent to him for a purpose. But more important, it has been demonstrated that good was there when he was ready to see it. If we wished to put this symbolically, we might say that a blessing came to him when his door opened to it.

Silas meets with the author's straightforward approval now. Godfrey, however, is still being treated with irony. It is not now comic irony, but is put in a more serious way. When he provides for Eppie and Silas, it is felt by Raveloe to be "nothing but right a man should be looked on and helped by those who could afford it, when he had brought up an orphan child and been father and mother to her...." It is still not known, of course, that Godfrey is the real father. A similar reminder of the past is that Eppie, knowing only Dolly Winthrop, feels that "a mother must be very precious." She does not know how different her own mother was.

Irony of another sort may be found in the news that Godfrey is having the Stone Pits drained. This irony rises from the contrast between what Godfrey intends in draining the waste land and what he achieves as a result. Even the reader cannot yet be sure that this is ironic, but there is a clear reminder of the frequent references to the pits when Dunstan was approaching Marner's cottage, and there is a preparation for the future.

Eliot's handling of Eppie offers both some of the best and some of the worst characterization in the book. It is difficult to present a relationship like that between Silas and Eppie, and difficult to portray a character as good as Eppie must be, for sentimentality is always only a step away. At times Eliot borders on the mire of sticky sweetness — for example, in showing Eppie with all her pets, or, earlier, with "Eppie in de toal-hole." It is a triumph that Eliot generally avoids this, that the life of Eppie and Silas is a relationship at once sweet, sincere, and believable.

The test of this comes when Eppie asks to marry Aaron: here there is a fine balance between care for her father and care for Aaron. The marriage will serve in another way as an index of character for both Silas and Eppie. It shows that Silas has reached the maturity of being able to share his treasure. In addition, by having marriage arranged now before Eppie finds out who she is, Eliot prepares a demonstration of Eppie's inner worth when she remains faithful to Aaron rather than choosing to become a lady, the daughter of Mr. and Mrs. Cass.

CHAPTERS 17–18

Summary

Priscilla and her father have gone home from church with Nancy and Godfrey. Nancy is trying to persuade them to stay for tea, but Priscilla thinks they must be getting home to look after the management of the farm. Her father now leaves everything to her management. Priscilla recommends that Nancy start a dairy to keep herself busy. Nancy says that that would not make up to Godfrey; but when Priscilla says that men want too much, Nancy defends her husband's disappointment at not having children.

After Priscilla leaves, Godfrey goes out to look at the draining of the Stone Pits, and Nancy sits alone and thinks over the years of their marriage. She asks herself whether she is to blame for Godfrey's disappointment. Their one child died in infancy, and when Godfrey had suggested that they adopt a child, she refused, saying that if they were meant to have a child one would have been granted them. Godfrey had wanted to adopt Eppie, and had pointed out that she seemed to have turned out well enough for Marner; but Nancy had pointed out that Marner didn't seek out the child. She was given to him. Nancy has always tried to make up to Godfrey in other ways his failure to have a family.

Godfrey has always specified that it should be Eppie whom they might adopt, but he has never been able to tell his wife why. He fears that she would feel only repulsion for him if she learned the truth. His childlessness has come to seem a retribution to him. It has never occurred to him that Marner might refuse to give up Eppie in any case, for his impressions of the feelings of laboring people are not very distinct.

Nancy's maid comes in with tea and reports that there is something strange going on outside. People are hurrying all one way on the road.

Nancy begins to feel an uncertain fear. She goes to the window to look for Godfrey, just as he enters at the other end of the room. He appears pale and shaken. He has her sit down before he tells her that Dunstan's skeleton has been found in the pits.

Nancy is somewhat surprised that Godfrey is so shaken by the death of a brother he cared little about. She thinks she understands his shame, when he says that Dunstan was the one who had robbed Silas. The money was found with him. Godfrey is not through, however. He says that the truth must come out sometime, and he tells her that Eppie is his own child. Nancy shows only regret when she replies that if he had told her that before, they could have done part of their duty to the child. Godfrey asks her forgiveness, but she says the wrong is not to her but to the child. Godfrey says that they may take the child now, then. They plan to go that evening to Marner's cottage.

Commentary

The beginning of Chapter 16 was a general view which included all the major characters. It then narrowed to Silas and brought his life up to date. Now the scene shifts to a comparable view of Godfrey and his family.

Changes may be noted here, but again they are changes of character which rise naturally from the personalities which were presented before and the events which have come between.

Priscilla was mannish before and is even more so now that she has carried out a man's job for many years. She talks like a man: she takes pleasure in "conquering the butter," if nothing greater; yet she has the characteristics of a woman and also fulfills a woman's part in caring for her father.

Mr. Lammeter is one of the few purely functional characters in the book. Unlike Squire Cass or Macey, he has no personality of his own, other than what local gossip has ascribed to him—pride and principle, mostly. He is a perpetual old man who serves as the father of Priscilla and Nancy, and that is all that is required.

Once again background information is quickly filled in. From Nancy's conversation with Priscilla we learn that she and Godfrey are childless. This also prepares us to examine both of their reactions to that fact. Nancy says that "another man 'ud hanker more than he does." Hence we know that Godfrey does want children, and that Nancy cares enough for him to defend him. This serves as an introduction to the examination of their marriage.

46

Godfrey and Nancy are related through their thoughts and a remembered conversation—related more closely than anyone has been except Silas and Eppie. These pages revolve around their mixed reactions to their childlessness. The movement is from Nancy's "Sunday thoughts" into a dramatic portrayal of a past scene (being remembered by her), through Godfrey's thoughts (as though Nancy were remembering them, too), and so back into Nancy's mind and then out into a portrayal of the present. This movement is complex but in no way confusing, and it explores thoroughly the exact nature of their marriage now.

Eliot partly explains Nancy's character and partly lets it be shown through her reminiscences. Basically Nancy has not changed. "The spirit of rectitude and the sense of responsibility for the effect of her conduct on others" are the center of her behavior; but a comparison of this reminiscence with her reactions in the past (for example, those at the New Year's dance) shows how much she has matured. This is shown even more clearly when we see that she is willing to bend a principle if she finds sympathy more important—as she does when Godfrey confesses that Eppie is his child. Nancy is more generous than Godfrey expects. Her sympathy for him is a measure of her maturity: Nancy as the young girl at the dance would never have been so generous. It is probably true that she wouldn't have married Godfrey if he had told her then.

We see that Godfrey has changed even less. Marriage with Nancy has strengthened his backbone, but not to the point that he feels able to voluntarily risk his happiness on a confession. He can easily find reasons for having what he wants. He is not unkind, but he still cannot imagine that anyone else has conflicting desires. However, a shock comes which changes even Godfrey somewhat, and the author prepares to make the most of it. She shows that "it seemed to him impossible that he should ever confess to her the truth about Eppie; she would never recover from the repulsion...." Knowing what he thinks he risks, it is more of a triumph that Godfrey finally is brought to confess. But he still lacks understanding. Once he has nothing further to hide, he is willing to face his duty but eager to talk about "rights." He assumes that he has a "right" to Eppie and that she and Silas will automatically agree.

CHAPTER 19

Summary

Silas and Eppie are at home alone that evening as Silas explains to her how he used to treasure his money before she came to him. Now he feels that the money was taken from him in time to save him, and it has been kept for him until it was wanted for her.

Godfrey and Nancy interrupt this talk. Godfrey begins by saying that he feels bound to make up for what a member of his family did to Silas. Then they speak of how little money Silas really has. At last Godfrey comes to the point of offering to raise Eppie as his daughter. Silas manages to reply that he will not stand in her way. Eppie, however, refuses politely, saying that she cannot leave her father. Godfrey has been anxious to set his error right, but now this block irritates him. He puts forth his claim on Eppie as his own child. Silas says angrily that Godfrey should have claimed her sixteen years ago, that repentance cannot change the events of sixteen years. Godfrey finally says that Silas should not stand in the way of the child's welfare. He wants to save her from marrying a workingman and leading a hard life forever. Silas then tells him to ask Eppie what she wants. Godfrey gently asks Eppie to come live with him, and Nancy also urges her. Eppie says she cannot be happy apart from Silas. When Silas asks her to consider carefully, she replies that she does not care to be a lady. Nancy then reminds Eppie that she has a duty to her real father; but Eppie feels no duty to any father but one, and she adds that she has already promised to marry a workingman. This closes the issue for Godfrey. He hurries away, followed by his wife.

Commentary

Silas was robbed by Dunstan; but the treasure which replaced his gold was Godfrey's daughter. Thus the two original plots become further interwoven, for now that Silas' gold has been returned, Godfrey feels able to claim his own. But he finds that this is not the sort of transaction which can be completed so neatly, for human feelings enter into it. He has neglected his duty, and in the process his "rights" as a father have vanished.

Godfrey suffered for his weakness in the past, but he kept his suffering to a minimum by refusing to face the cause. He still has not faced the issue, for he is not yet concerned with Eppie, but with himself. "He had been full of his own penitence and resolution to retrieve his error...." Now he is baffled, because Eppie does not want to be "retrieved." That he has no concept of what his daughter wants is shown by his fear that "she may marry some low working man." This is just what Eppie desires.

Nancy is in a difficult position. She believes in "principle," and by that belief Eppie is Godfrey's. She also loves her husband and wishes to protect him. For these reasons she partly takes his position and his narrow point of view: "We shall want for nothing when we have our daughter." She too speaks of "a duty you owe to your lawful father." But it is implied that she does so out of concern for Godfrey rather than from conviction.

The author views the action from the point of view of each of the participants in turn in order to give the fullest sense of what is happening. But she concentrates on two characters – Silas and Eppie. Certainly they are the ones who are intended to have the "right" feelings, and their views are put most forcefully. We have already seen what sort of life Nancy and Godfrey have achieved. Now the relationship of Silas and Eppie is tested more deeply than ever and found to be sound. It is deeper than Godfrey imagines, or even Nancy. It shows the full extent of Silas' "salvation."

Silas, compared to Godfrey, has suffered more greatly; but he has come to maturity and through that to his reward. He is willing to sacrifice his own interests for Eppie's sake; but she refuses her part in that bargain.

Silas is right in telling Godfrey that "repentance doesn't alter what's been going on for sixteen years." Fatherhood is more than blood; it is a carefully built relationship that cannot be given or stolen like gold. Even principle – Godfrey's "duty" – cannot overcome the claims of love. The central irony of Godfrey's position is now brought home to him: because of his past weakness he can never have his desire. In the end his weakness brings its own punishment.

CHAPTER 20

Summary

At home Godfrey and Nancy agree that they cannot now alter their daughter's upbringing. Godfrey sees that there are debts which cannot be put off and paid later. He decides that there is no reason now to let it be known that Eppie is his daughter. Nancy, thinking of Priscilla and her father, agrees. Godfrey thinks, however, that he will put it in his will. He guesses that it is Aaron she means to marry, and he decides to help her in any way he can. He realizes that Eppie has taken a dislike to him, but he considers that part of his punishment. But in spite of his disappointments, some good has come of the matter, for he knows now how lucky he is to have Nancy as his wife.

Commentary

The attempt to reclaim his daughter has been Godfrey's last test, the one which brings him a realization of the nature of human contacts – "there's debts we can't pay like money debts...." The contrast between Eppie and the gold is continued in that statement; and a moment later the image of Eppie as a blessing is renewed. Godfrey realizes at last that he has turned away a blessing, that while he wanted to "pass for childless" once, he must ironically be childless now.

Godfrey views his childlessness as punishment. In a sense this is gratuitous poetic justice, for his childlessness does not rise from the error he is being punished for. However, it is appropriate, and it is not the sole cause of his remorse. Even before he married Nancy, Godfrey felt guilty about not claiming Eppie. His failure to have other children is only an addition to that. In thinking of this as divine retribution Godfrey is only sharing a belief common to the characters of the novel. It is not, however, a belief to which the author commits herself.

Godfrey often makes bad impressions, but Eliot always softens them in the end. In this case the effect of the preceding chapter is softened by a view of Godfrey and Nancy alone together. If their love does not extend to the depth of Silas and Eppie's, still theirs is a successful marriage, and with one another they are generous and thoughtful. Godfrey can rightly find some consolation in the thought that he has Nancy "in spite of all." Furthermore, he now for the first time displays some decisiveness in doing his duty even when it goes against his desire — he determines to help Eppie and Aaron even though he did not want her to marry a workingman.

CHAPTER 21

Summary

The next day Silas tells Eppie that he has decided to take a trip back to his old home. He wants to talk to Mr. Paston, the minister, about the robbery and the drawing of lots. Eppie is delighted, for she thinks this journey will give her at least one small advantage over Aaron, who is so much wiser than she in most things.

When Silas asks her, Dolly agrees that he should go, for she thinks it will make his mind easier.

On the fourth day following, Silas and Eppie arrive in his old town. It has changed so that he hardly knows his way. He has to ask directions to Lantern Yard. The only landmark he recognizes is the old prison. All the streets have changed. The walls are grimy and the people sallow-faced and dirty. When at last he comes to where the Yard should be, Silas finds in its place a factory. No one knows anything of the chapel or the minister.

When he returns to Raveloe Silas tells Dolly that the past will be dark to the last. Dolly agrees, but she adds that the fact that he will never know the "rights" of the matter doesn't mean that no right exists. With that Silas feels bound to agree.

50

Commentary

"Now the money's been brought back," Silas feels able to return to Lantern Yard to seek for the truth of his past. This is not merely a matter of economics; his feeling is not only that he can afford the trip, but that now he is inwardly capable of seeking the truth about the past. Religion is one of the problems he wants to resolve — to settle his doubts about the conflicts between his old faith and his new one. This very process of doubting is a measure of his development: in the past he first believed "unquestioned doctrine" and then rejected all doctrines.

The name Lantern Yard has taken on an ironic tinge now. Dolly asks Silas to bring back "any light to be got up the yard as you talk on, we've need of it i' this world...." Lantern Yard was a light for Silas once, but that went out long ago and it cannot be rekindled now. He finds everything changed, and the only thing to cheer him is the sight of a prison. Silas wants to set everything in his life to rights, but that is beyond his power.

Lantern Yard is in darkness both literally and symbolically. Prison Street remains, dark and ugly; pale faces stare out from gloomy doorways; there is a bad smell in the air. This was a common enough physical condition among nineteenth-century factories, and as such this scene helps fill out the social background of the novel. But it is also like the evil darkness that must remain a part of Silas' past.

Dolly is convinced that there was some good, some rightness, in the past, despite the apparent injustice: "...that doesn't hinder there *being* a rights, Master Marner, for all it's dark to you and me." Silas' faith is more tentative, but he has certainly arrived at a kind of faith. All his life he has depended on some support — his religion, his gold, his daughter. He never becomes quite independent, but at last he has a secure prop. He says he will "trusten" till he dies, now that Eppie has said she will never leave him; but even that is not his real support. It is within himself, his own love for another; for, as he says, "Since the time the child was sent to me and I've come to love her as myself, I've had light enough to trusten by...." In a letter, George Eliot wrote that "the idea of God...is the ideal of a goodness entirely human." Through his troubles Silas has become convinced that there is goodness in other men and in himself, and that is the basis of his faith.

There is one fine touch of characterization which should be noted. Eppie is delighted at the chance of a trip with Silas so that she may have at least one advantage over Aaron. This small touch of ambition gives a moment's relief from Eppie's eternal sweetness, but without detracting from that sweetness. It is a humanizing touch which both broadens her character and seems natural to it. Such small touches as this are a mark of Eliot's skill as a novelist.

CONCLUSION

Summary

Eppie is married on a morning when the lilacs are blooming and the sun shining. Her gown was provided by Mrs. Godfrey Cass. Mr. Cass is unfortunately out of town on the day of the wedding. Priscilla Lammeter, coming to keep her sister company, sees the bridal party and wishes that Nancy could have found a child like that.

The bridal party is seen by the humbler part of the village, too. Old Mr. Macey proclaims that he has lived to see his words come true, for Silas has got his money back, and rightfully so. The party of guests at the Rainbow are already assembled, and they have joined in agreement that Silas has brought a blessing on himself by being a father to an orphan.

Commentary

The author's use of nature images has been noted earlier. The whole environment sometimes reflects a character's reaction to his situation or his relationship with humanity. Recall the darkness and rain which accompanied Dunstan, the darkness which had fallen on Lantern Yard. Here sunshine is the harbinger of happiness for Eppie and Aaron, as well as for Silas.

Important imagery is continued in other ways: Eppie's hair is a "dash of gold"; she is dressed in pure white, recalling that she was once pictured as a "white-winged angel."

The relationship with Godfrey is brought into its final focus. It is apparent that Godfrey still feels some pain for his daughter, for he has found reason to be out of town. The truth is still not known in Raveloe, however, and that ignorance is made the source of a double irony. Raveloe thinks the most important part of Godfrey's feeling is that Silas "had been wronged by one of his own family." This is true, but the guilty party is not the one they think of. This is followed by a more personal reference from Priscilla: "I could ha' wished Nancy had had the luck to find a child like that and bring her up...." Priscilla's more intimate knowledge coupled with an ignorance equal to the villagers' gives a new angle of irony.

A final word is heard from the chorus, mainly in the persons of Macey and the farrier. Community sentiment toward Silas is summed up in the general feeling "that he had brought a blessing on himself." For once there is no contradiction.

CHARACTER ANALYSES

SILAS MARNER

Silas is in no way a heroic character. He is not notably intelligent or courageous or unselfish. He is a product of Eliot's desire to arouse sympathy for ordinary imperfect humanity going about its day-to-day business.

Silas changes greatly during the course of the book; yet part of him always remains "the same Silas Marner who had once loved his fellow with tender love and trusted in an unseen goodness." That original love and trust seemed crushed by the evils which befall him, but they return with even greater strength, and it seems natural that they should do so. The changes in Silas' character are never arbitrary. They have roots; they develop naturally from his past. The betrayal by William Dane costs Silas his faith in men, and the betrayal of the drawing of the lots takes his faith in a just God. The second robbery sets in place of the just God a vision of a "cruel power." Yet because he does believe in a power, Silas is able to believe that Eppie is sent for his salvation; and through Eppie's influence he finds new faith in the goodness of other men.

The unchanging part of Silas' character is that which requires some prop on which he can lean, something to support his courage to face life. When he loses his religion, he turns to his work, and then to his gold. When his gold is gone, he finds a better support in a child. This leads ultimately to his faith in his fellow men and in his own strength.

Silas is always honest, both with himself and with others. He is unable to question the rightness of church doctrine, and he will not easily believe that William would betray him. Later he cannot force himself to imagine anything suspicious about the strange peddler even when he wishes to believe that the man might have been the thief. But while he retains some good qualities, he loses his sympathy for men, and then all his affections are in danger of withering away. He becomes almost dead to the world. But when he appears in the final pages as a man with new faith, he has not been merely restored to his original position. He has gained maturity and inner strength. He has the courage to give up his daughter, his treasure, for her good. His faith is not based on unquestioned doctrine; rather, it survives in spite of doubts. His is no overwhelming triumph, but a believable, human one.

NANCY LAMMETER

Nancy, like Silas, changes during the course of the story. However, her change is not the apparent result of the force of events. Rather it is the realization of something which was inherent in her, a simple process of maturing. It is none the less believable for that.

Nancy as a young girl is charming and graceful. This the author brings home by demonstration—by portrayal of her actions—by the testimony of other characters, and by narration. Nancy is also shown to have high and strict principles: she does not care to associate with any man of poor reputation. It might be feared that her principles will become too strict with time, except that her character already has the saving touch of emotion. Despite her resolves she cannot entirely overcome her love for Godfrey.

Part of Nancy's youthful "principle" is girlish self-dramatization. When this disappears with her maturity, it leaves a base of real principle, but it is sweetened by love which can become sympathy. Nancy's principle keeps her from adopting a child, but her love for Godfrey makes her try to make it up to him in other ways. When she discovers that Eppie is Godfrey's own daughter, it is not the principle which governs her actions, as Godfrey had feared, but the love and sympathy. The insight into her character which has been given through the scenes presented from her point of view has prepared for this development. It is a surprise only to Godfrey.

GODFREY CASS

Godfrey's character is summed up by the author near the beginning as "irresolution and moral cowardice." This is the state in which he continues until almost the end. Godfrey is not evil in any way. He has no desire to harm anyone; he is pained when he does so. But he has not the courage to take responsibility for his acts nor to give up his desires when they conflict with duty.

Eliot is careful to make excuses for Godfrey. The early marriage was not really his fault; he has good intentions about caring for Eppie; he really wants to lead a better life. Yet these are only the ultimate complication of Godfrey's situation. Such "excuses" are an insufficient defense. Godfrey knows that, and Eliot tries to make sure that the reader does too. She seems to be saying that there are times when wrong can be made to seem almost right, but that such conditions provide a weak base for a life.

Godfrey's life with Nancy sets him on a better path, but there is no true test of his character except his failure to own Eppie as his daughter. This shows that Godfrey is unchanged — he wants to do the right things, but not badly enough to risk his happiness. In the end he tells the truth only because he is afraid it will be found out anyway. His own desires still are the most important thing to him. He puts them in the form of principle now — he thinks he has a "right" to his daughter, although he was willing to neglect the corresponding duty.

Godfrey at last comes to some self-realization. The unexpected resistance he meets from Silas and Eppie brings home to him for the first time the fact that rights and duties cannot be separated. He accepts his rebuke willingly. Still, he fails to do his whole duty. He takes the easy way out, deciding to "own" Eppie only in his will. But at least he does it from better motives, from consideration for others rather than for himself.

EPPIE

Eppie is the least developed of the major characters. This is to be expected: hers is a functional role, and it hardly requires a fully characterized individual to fulfill it. During half the time she is in the story, she is a small child. There is no attempt to make her a special sort of child, except in Silas' eyes. She has the normal child's habits and a childish cuteness. This is sufficient for her function, which to that point is only to bring Silas into contact with his neighbors.

As a young woman Eppie has a more difficult part. In order to show the sort of life Silas has achieved, it is necessary for Eppie to have some semblance of a personality. However, there is little time in which to achieve any complexity of character. Eliot takes some pains to give Eppie depth by showing incidents which are emblematic of her character, rather than by providing a full background of her life. Thus Eppie's fondness for animals stands for all of her affectionate nature. She is put in the position of having to choose between her two "fathers," and this demonstrates that her affection has depth. A small touch of complexity is given by her wish to have one slight advantage over Aaron.

In the end Eppie is most important for the effect her presence has on Silas' life and on Godfrey's. The character she is given is suited to her functional role, but it does not go far beyond that.

DUNSTAN CASS

Dunstan is set as a direct contrast to Godfrey. Where Godfrey is merely weak, Dunstan is bad all the way. He is vain, arrogant, and selfish, as well as dishonest. Like Godfrey, he is primarily interested in what he himself wants, but he lacks any saving virtues. Dunstan suspects his own worthlessness: while he thinks what a fine person he is, he fears the opinions of others on that subject. This is put symbolically by having Dunstan take Godfrey's whip, as it gives a better appearance than his own.

Dunstan, like Eppie, is just the sort of person needed to fulfill his role. He serves as a contrast to Godfrey, as a means of relieving Silas of his gold, and as a reminder to Godfrey that truth will out. When not needed he can be conveniently removed from the story without being missed. He is an example of static characterization—he shows no development during the story, but comes on the scene full-blown. However, he has a certain complexity: his repressed knowledge of his faults gives him a psychological interest that Eppie lacks.

THE CHORAL CHARACTERS

Macey, Dowlas, Snell, Lundy, Tookey, Winthrop

This group of characters represents the range of Raveloe character and opinion, from Macey, the self-admiring authoritative old-timer, to Tookey, the defensively uncertain newcomer. Dowlas is the "negative spirit" of the group, almost a freethinker. Snell, the landlord, is the peacemaker; while Ben Winthrop is simply an average well-established inhabitant of Raveloe. None of the group is developed to any depth, but they are distinct individuals. Some of them—Macey and Dowlas especially—are among the more forceful characters of the book. As a group they give information about the background of the story, comment on the action, and are a source of broad comedy.

DOLLY WINTHROP

She has an instinctive faith which contrasts with Silas' initial distrust of Heaven. She represents the best of Raveloe, the community spirit and real interest and concern for others. She is no stereotype; through her discussions with Silas she reveals a full personality, slow in thought but steady in faith and strong in her sympathy.

CRITICAL ANALYSIS

PLOT AND STRUCTURE

The book covers a long span of time—over thirty years. However, concentration within this span limits the time actually portrayed to three relatively short periods. The first of these, the time on which the book opens, shows Silas living his lonely existence at Raveloe. This is followed by a flashback to the time fifteen years earlier when he was driven from Lantern Yard. The time then skips quickly back to its original point, settling on a November afternoon. The events between then and New Year's take up the first portion of the book, although the narrator briefly mentions some events which follow as Silas begins to raise Eppie.

Sixteen years are then jumped over, and the results of the early events are seen. The intervening years are filled in mostly by the narrator or by conversations between characters. There are only a few brief dramatic portrayals of events during those years—for example, Godfrey and Nancy's discussion about adopting Eppie. After the past is brought up to date, the time remains at the same Sunday on which this portion of the book opened, until the main plot considerations are disposed of (for example, Dunstan's disappearance, Godfrey's relationship to Eppie, and Eppie's future). Some events occur after that—Silas goes to Lantern Yard a few days later, and still later Eppie is married—but they are treated very briefly.

The three times on which the author concentrates contain five main events: the Lantern Yard robbery, the theft of Silas' gold, the death of Molly (or the arrival of Eppie), the return of Silas' gold, and Godfrey's attempt to claim his child.

Consideration of these basic events gives a broad view of the structure of *Silas Marner*. They are all more or less related, either in the mind of one or more characters, or by cause-and-effect. The last four fall into pairs: the theft of the gold and the coming of Eppie in its place; the return of the gold and Godfrey's claim on Eppie. The first two are not related in fact, as the reader knows; but Silas and the other inhabitants of Raveloe consider them to be a kind of cause-and-effect; and this gives rise to a symbolic relationship between them. The latter pair are related strictly through their cause—the discovery of Dunstan's body with the gold leads Godfrey to confess that he is Eppie's father. But the symbolic relationship which has been established carries over from the past. The first event, the robbery at Lantern Yard, is of course the indirect cause of the rest, for it sends Silas to Raveloe; but it also provides the basis for Silas' reactions at the time of the second robbery—it causes his feeling of being tormented by an unseen power. As such it is responsible for the symbolic values of later events.

There are two plots in *Silas Marner:* there is Silas' rejection of humanity and his redemption; and there is the plot involving Godfrey and his two wives. The two plots are not unrelated, however. In the beginning there is little connection between them; but by the end of the tale they are inseparable. A glance at the events outlined above shows how this happens. The structure of the book might be thought of as a funnel, with Godfrey and Silas on opposite sides at first but gradually being carried by events into the same course. There are many parallels between their lives. At first these parallels are distant, but they come closer and closer until at last they join. Note, for example, that Godfrey is betrayed by Dunstan as Silas was betrayed by William Dane. Godfrey has two wives to correspond to Silas' two treasures; in both cases the first is their ruin, while the second is their salvation. Their first real connection is the gold: Dunstan is trying to extort money from Godfrey, and when he fails at that he steals it from Silas. Eppie comes to replace the gold, and she is the second and far closer connection between Silas and Godfrey. Godfrey is her real father, but Silas becomes like a father to her. Furthermore, the event which brings Eppie to Silas is looked on as a blessing by both Silas and Godfrey, for it frees Godfrey to marry Nancy.

The meaning of the novel and its symbolic values are completely bound up in the contrasts and comparisons between these two plots. The nature of a "blessing," the meaning of good and bad in relation to social conduct — these and other problems become involved in the working out of events. Nor are Godfrey and Silas the only persons involved. Their lives are connected most of all through the society in which they live. The community of Raveloe is an agent of their acts as well as a spectator and commentator. When Silas discovers the robbery, he reports it to the Rainbow, and Godfrey hears of it from there. A cross-section of the community is present to receive word of Molly's death. Eppie provides a connecting link not only between Godfrey and Silas, but between Silas and the community as well. Communal opinion is never the final authority in the novel; Eliot often treats it ironically; but it is an important factor in the lives of the major characters and in the functioning of the plot.

TECHNIQUE AND CHARACTERIZATION

Like most novelists of her day, Eliot uses an omniscient point of view — that is, she views the action from any point she finds convenient, whether from the narrator's standpoint, as a disinterested spectator might see it, or as seen or felt by any character. This has many advantages, and it is well suited to Eliot's strengths as a novelist. It allows her to show what any character thinks or feels and to show an act and its consequences with great comprehensiveness. Eliot uses this technique to increase the reader's sympathy and understanding of characters and of the situations they find themselves in. It also allows better control of the reader's awareness, which is the main source of the irony so important in Eliot's novels. The reader generally knows more than any single character (for example, he knows about Godfrey's marriage and that Dunstan is the thief), and this superior knowledge lends ironic humor to the things the characters think and do in their ignorance. However, the reader is not told everything. The news of Dunstan's death is perhaps less of a surprise to him than to Godfrey, but it has never been a certainty. This allows the reader to feel something of the shock which Godfrey must feel at that moment.

The excellence of Eliot's characterization depends partly on this omniscience, but the most important factor is Eliot's deep understanding of human psychology. Her major characters are portrayed in great depth. Their reactions are varied; they are capable of surprising; yet they never seem arbitrary. On reflection, that which seemed surprising in them is seen to be consistent with their previous actions. They do not remain static, but their development builds on the past. A prime example of this is Silas. His belief in God goes through a series of developments which are directly related to the things which have happened to him. Throughout all these changes, however, he clings to some support—his church, his work, his gold, or his daughter. His character displays both change and constancy, and this makes him recognizably the same person even as he changes. His character does not merely change—it develops.

Eliot's style lends her several aids to characterization. The omniscient point of view sometimes does this by giving the reaction of an unprejudiced observer, someone whom the reader will believe. The Miss Gunns find Nancy charming; and since they are neutral toward her at best, the reader is likely to accept their view. Another important device of persuasion is metaphor. These are likely to go almost unperceived by the reader, but they have a cumulative effect. Throughout the first chapters Silas is compared to a spider in a number of ways, and this "insect-like existence" lends reality to the withering of his humanity. A third device of characterization is speech. The characters do not all talk alike. Squire Cass's speech is rough but forceful. Priscilla sounds almost like a man, and from what we see of her it is evident that she is trying to fill a man's place. All of the characters except Godfrey speak a more or less rustic dialect, but it is more pronounced when the author is calling attention to the insularity of the community—for example, at the gathering at the Rainbow. Godfrey's speech is always somewhat more refined than his neighbors' or his father's, indicating perhaps that he is at least trying to hold himself above a life of "conviviality and condescension."

THEMES

Themes are simply ideas which the author develops in the course of the novel. It should be remembered, however, that what a good novel *says* is not detachable from the way it says it. The meaning is a part of the style and structure, and themes cannot be set out in so many pointed quotations. Meanings and attitudes are expressed through the whole work of art, and they must be studied as a part of it.

The major theme of *Silas Marner* is of course the influence of "pure, natural human relationships"; but there are several others. Some of these are never the subject of a direct statement, but constant repetition brings them to the reader's attention, and the novel draws some sort of conclusion about them. One of these themes is the function of religion in society. Another is the use of custom and tradition. There is a more direct consideration, focused on Nancy, of the extent to which "principle" should predominate over sympathy in human relationships. This is closely connected to the question of indulgence versus discipline in human life, as exemplified by the home life of Godfrey and of Nancy.

A theme may be mentioned only indirectly and yet be quite explicit in its meaning. One such in *Silas Marner* is the effect of industrialization on English society in the nineteenth century. Lantern Yard after the factory has been built is a grimy, dark place full of unhealthy people. There is a sharp contrast between the grim unfriendliness of Lantern Yard and the community spirit of Raveloe, between Silas' life as a spinning insect and the fresh air of the open fields.

SYMBOLISM

A symbol is an object which demands attention in itself but which also refers to another object or to a concept. Normal images and metaphors, through consistent use, may become symbols. Symbols may operate in more than one way at the same time, and often there is no one concept attached to a given object; but instead a whole range of ideas may be brought into play. The tale of Silas Marner certainly must be understood symbolically as well as literally. Eppie is explicitly put forward as a substitute for Silas' treasure, and this raises questions of the nature of treasures literal and spiritual. Dunstan steals Silas' gold and in the process falls into a pit; but in another way this may be thought of as the pit which waits for all erring men. Silas' door stands open as a symbol of his spiritual condition; and evil and good in turn come and work their influence on him. Silas' renewal of faith and human contact in this way becomes a symbolic rebirth; both through his fits and through his alienation from other men he is a man who has seemed dead and has come back to life.

QUESTIONS FOR REVIEW

1. Discuss Eliot's use of Biblical allusions and their function in the novel.
2. What sort of dramatic or thematic unity do you find in the tale of Silas Marner?
3. Discuss the various ways in which the author portrays or develops characters.
4. Contrast the methods used to characterize Silas and Mr. Macey.
5. Does the author express any personal religious beliefs through this novel? How does religion affect the lives of the characters?
6. Aside from Silas' visit to Lantern Yard, does the novel offer any comment on contemporary industrial conditions?
7. *Silas Marner* is frequently referred to as a "fairy tale." What fairy tale elements does it have? Does the label fit?
8. Discuss Eliot's use of comic irony.
9. Is coincidence overworked in the plot of *Silas Marner*?
10. What is the purpose of introducing the peddler as a suspect in the robbery?
11. Do you think the novel would be more effective if the author did not intrude in the story?
12. Compare the technique or style of *Silas Marner* to that of any other novel by George Eliot.
13. "No man can begin to mould himself on a faith or an idea without rising to a higher order of experience." Apply this statement by Eliot to *Silas Marner*.
14. Can Silas' final view of life be reconciled with life as Godfrey experiences it?
15. Do you think *Silas Marner* was written to make a philosophical point?

SELECTED BIBLIOGRAPHY

Bennet, Joan. *George Eliot, Her Mind and Her Art.* London: Cambridge University Press, 1948. A competent biography combined with penetrating essays on the individual novels.

Cecil, David. *Victorian Novelists: Essays in Revaluation.* New York: Bobbs-Merrill Co., 1935. Also in paperback, Phoenix Books Edition; Chicago: University of Chicago Press, 1958. A fine general introduction to the work of Eliot (and other nineteenth-century novelists) and her place in the development of the English novel.

Haight, Gordon S. *The George Eliot Letters.* Yale University Press, 1952-56. A firsthand source of Eliot's life and ideas, it includes her journals and letters by and to her. Volume III covers the period of *Silas Marner*.

Hardy, Barbara. *The Novels of George Eliot*. London: The Athlone Press, 1959. A study in depth of Eliot's novels using the principles of the "new criticism."

Harvey, W. J. *The Art of George Eliot*. New York: Oxford University Press, 1962. Offers sound critical thinking on the individual novels.

Leavis, F. R. *The Great Tradition*. London: Chatto and Windus, 1948. A study of Eliot, Henry James, and Joseph Conrad. This influential book is the take-off point for a great deal of subsequent Eliot criticism. It offers only a brief and rather unsatisfactory treatment of *Silas Marner*, however.

Stang, Richard, ed. *Discussions of George Eliot*. Boston: Heath and Co., 1960. A good, well-edited selection of commentary by Eliot's contemporaries and later authors and critics. It contains selections from other works listed here and offers a valuable cross-section of reaction to Eliot's works.

Thale, Jerome. *The Novels of George Eliot*. New York: Columbia University Press, 1959. A thoughtful and original examination of the novels. The section on *Silas Marner* is perhaps weaker than the rest, but the book as a whole is one of the more valuable critical works available.

Willey, Basil. *Nineteenth Century Studies: Coleridge to Matthew Arnold*. New York: Columbia University Press, 1949. Discusses Eliot's nonfictional works and her place in the nineteenth-century history of ideas.

NOTES

Your Guides to Successful Test Preparation.

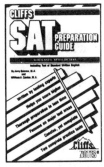  

Cliffs Test Preparation Guides

Efficient preparation means better test scores. Go with the experts and use **Cliffs Test Preparation Guides**. They'll help you reach your goals because they're: • Complete • Concise • Functional • In-depth. They are focused on helping you know what to expect from each test. The test-taking techniques have been proven in classroom programs nationwide.

Recommended for individual use or as a part of formal test preparation programs.